PARTY DIVAS!

12 Fabulous Parties for Women's Ministry

Amber Van Schooneveld

party: a group assembled for amusement or celebration

divas: a term originally used to describe women of rare, outstanding talent

Let's get Ready to Party!

Incredible things will happen™

Loveland, CO
www.group.com

Spring

"Always a Bridesmaid" Brunch p. 22

Every woman has one lurking in the dark recesses of her closet. Tell your girlfriends to dust off those old prom, bridesmaid, wedding, or mother-of-the-bride dresses. It's time for a lighthearted spring brunch where women will laugh while reliving old memories and deepening friendships.

Candied Rose Petals

Cantaloupe Soup

Menu

- Roasted Asparagus Bundles
  with Maple Dijon Cream Sauce
- Wild Mushroom Quiche
- Chilled Cantaloupe Soup
- Strawberry Phyllo Cups
- Rhubarb Strawberry Cooler

Strawberry
Phyllo Cups

I Love Paris in the Springtime : p. 30

Cobblestone streets, sidewalk cafes, market days…Even if we've never been, we all love Paris in the springtime. This "just because" party will treat you and your friends as you simply enjoy life! You'll experience a cheese tasting while speaking in the best French accent you can muster. Step aside, Inspector Clouseau.

Crème Brûlée

Menu

- Really *French Onion Soup*
- *Lemon Tarragon Scallops*
- *Simple Green Salad*
- *Cheese Tasting*
- *Crème Brûlée*

Une fois, j'ai mange vingt beignets en deux minutes ndant un pari.

Mes talons n'arretent pas de se coincer dans les cailloux.

Spring

Feast of Esther : p. 36

Hamentaschen Cookies

Celebrate the exuberant holiday of Purim, a Jewish holiday commemorating the brave actions of one woman and God's protection of his people. You'll have a costume contest, a melodrama of Esther's story, and pray for God's people who are persecuted today.

Challah Bread

Make sure to get cozy, Persian style!

Menu

- *Challah Bread*
- *Cucumber Salad*
- *Apricot Chicken with Almond Raisin Rice Pilaf*
- *Bread, Cheese, and Herb Plate*
- *Hamentaschen*

Market Day in Tuscany : p. 42

Panzanella & Prosciutto-Wrapped Shrimp

Bright yellow sunflowers, bursting red tomatoes, fresh fragrant basil. Have a market day Italian party that brings all of the delights of the Tuscan countryside to your table. Lingering at the table with good food and good friends…ah, la Vita e bella!

Menu

- *Balsamic-Glazed Pearl Onions*
- *Panzanella*
- *Prosciutto-Wrapped Shrimp*
- *Italian Cheese Platter*
- *Fresh Peaches with Mascarpone Cream and Amaretti*

Summer

Let's Go Fly a Kite: Freedom Picnic p. 48

This picnic at the park is a great time for you to celebrate your own freedom with your friends, while fighting for the freedom of women around the globe in this easy service project.

Menu

- *Pressed Sandwich Italiano*
- *Sweet Corn Zucchini Boats*
- *Watermelon Pops*
- *the Best Oatmeal Cookies*
- *Pucker-Up Punch*

Southwest Cowgirl Campfire ⋮ p. 54

Put on your spurs! Nothing's better than a night under the stars with a campfire and some friends. Enjoy those great outdoors—even if it's just your backyard!

Make sure your girlfriends put on their boots!

Menu

- *Mint Limeade*
- *Baked Tortilla Chips with the Fastest Guac in the West*
- *Green Chili Buffalo Burgers*
- *Grilled Corn on the Cob With Santa Fe Spice Butter*
- *Grilled Cinnamon Peaches*
- *Cinnamon and Coffee Terrine With Mexican Chocolate Ganache*

The Great Adventure Party : p. 62

Aam ki Kulfi

How daring are *you*? Get ready for an evening of adventure with your friends. You'll brave new heights and stir the embers of adventure God has placed in each person's soul.

Brightly-colored pillar candles accent your decorations!

Menu

- Es Alpukat (Mocha Avocado Chiller)
- North African Tomato Soup
- B'stilla (Moroccan Chicken Pastry)
- Moroccan-Spiced Carrots
- Aam ki Kulfi (Indian Mango Ice Cream)

Make your dining experience an adventure!

Fall

Murder at Kensington Manor : p. 69

Host your very own murder mystery night. Women will not only solve a mystery, but also unravel the truth of God's pursuit of them.

Dust off those fancy dishes and decorations!

Ask and it will be given to you; seek and you will find; knock and the door will be opened to you.
Luke 11:9

Menu

- *Spiced Cider*
- *Creamy Butternut Bisque*
- *Rosemary Pork Tenderloin With Apple Cream Sauce*
- *Rosemary Roasted Potatoes*
- *Gingerbread Pumpkin Trifle With Maple Whipped Cream and Candied Pecans*

In Grandma's Kitchen : p. 75

Prepare for the holidays by learning some good ol' home-making skills together. Learn how to make a perfect pie crust and knit Christmas gifts as you cozy in from the cold together.

Menu
- Ginger Snap's Hot Cocoa
- Dottie Mae's Artichoke Dip
- Jan's Creamy Chicken Noodle Soup
- Thelma Mae's Angel Biscuits
- Delma's Herbed Green Bean Casserole
- Aunt Cin's Apple Pie

Have your girlfriends wear their coziest clothes!

Candy Cane Brunch : p. 81

We all love Christmas parties—but who has time to plan in December? This simple brunch will make your holiday party together a breeze, not a burden.

A peppermint stick & rose centerpiece— how lovely!

Dried Cherries & Dates

Menu

- *Eggnog Pancakes*
- *Christmas Morning Casserole*
- *Baked Apples With Cinnamon Stems*
- *Candy Cane Snowballs*
- *Chai Nog/Chocolate Nog*

"Girls Just Wanna Have Fun" Pajama Party! : p. 86

You've gotta try this!

Pizza, pillow fights, face masks, Truth or Dare. You'll laugh like schoolgirls while discovering truths about yourselves and one another. *Warning: Excessive giggling may ensue.*

Break out the candy bling!

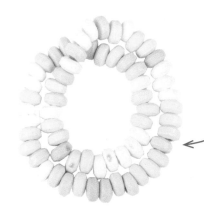

Menu

- *Veggies and Cheese Dip*
- *California Pizza*
- *Tara's Strawberry Salad*
- *Apple Pie Shakes*
- *Chrissy's Morning After Frappe*

Girl-About-Town Cosmopolitan Bash : p. 91

It's time for those little black dresses. Get your girlfriends together for a night of sophistication as you experience culture and haute cuisine at your pad. Then it's off to the art galleries or a night of exploring expressions of faith.

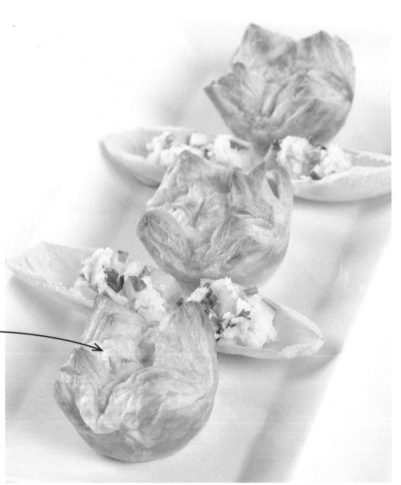

Mmm...who knew chic tasted so good?

Menu

- Cuban Spritzer
- Finger Food
- Toasted Ravioli
- Crab and Mango Bites
- Onion and Camembert Tarts
- Honey Tasting
- Poached Pears With Chocolate Sauce

"There was some one thing that was too great for God to show us when he walked upon our earth; and I have sometimes fancied that it was His mirth."

—G.K. Chesterton, *Orthodoxy*

. . . .

Dedication

To my taste-tester, fellow-dreamer, friend, and love, Michael

Special Thanks

to Amy Nappa, whose generous support and encouragement resulted in this book,

to Jan Kershner, my talented editor (*and* a great cook),

to Andrea Filer and Samantha Wranosky for making my book look so darn good,

and to all my friends and family who helped with recipes and ate my food.

Party Divas! 12 Fabulous Parties for Women's Ministry

Visit our Web site: **www.group.com**

Credits
Author: Amber Van Schooneveld
Chief Creative Officer: Joani Schultz
Senior Developer: Amy Nappa
Editor: Jan Kershner
Assistant Editor: Dena Twinem
Art Director: Andrea Filer
Book and Cover Designer: Samantha Wranosky
Print Production Artist: Samantha Wranosky
Photographer: Rodney Stewart
Food Stylists: Jacqueline Buckner, Andrea Filer, and Samantha Wranosky
Illustrators: Samantha Wranosky and Veronica Lucas
Production Manager: DeAnne Lear

 Library of Congress Cataloging-in-Publication Data
Van Schooneveld, Amber, 1978-
 Party divas! : 12 fabulous parties for women's ministry / Amber Van Schooneveld ; [edited by Jan Kershner].
    p. cm.
 ISBN 978-0-7644-3487-7 (pbk. : alk. paper)
 1. Church work with women. 2. Parties--Religious aspects--Christianity. I. Kershner, Jan. II. Title.
 BV4445.V36 2007
 259.082--dc22
                            2007028165

ISBN 978-0-7644-3487-7

10 9 8 7 6 5 4 3 2 1   17 16 15 14 13 12 11 10 09 08
Printed in the United States of America.

Table of Contents

Introduction

"Rejoice in the Lord always. I will say it again: Rejoice!"
Philippians 4:4

You've heard the old saying "Eat, drink, and be merry, for tomorrow we die!" Well here's a new one: *Eat, drink, and be merry, for today we live!* As Christians, we have some serious reasons for partying: God loves us. God reached out to us and saved us. God gave us one another to embrace life together. We live to glorify God, and, as the above verse says, that's reason to rejoice. *Always.*

Celebrations are times we stop, put all of the incidentals cluttering our minds to the side, and focus on one of the truest purposes in life: worshipping and celebrating God with one another. This book can help you and your girlfriends not only de-stress and have a good time, but also fulfill one of your greatest purposes!

And because we are to rejoice *always*, this book includes one party for each month. You can use them however you like: a quiet evening with a couple of close friends, a wild and crazy church-wide women's event, a non-threatening party for your friends who've never been to church, a time to grow deeper spiritually with a small group. You can even adapt them to invite your family or the men along.

Here's what you'll get:

Party Tip

These recipes are meant to be fabulous, so some of the ingredients may be unfamiliar to you. Trying something new will be an adventure! Grocery stores carry more than you think, so be sure to ask your grocer where to find items you're not familiar with. You'll be glad you did—you might just discover a new favorite ingredient!

Menus

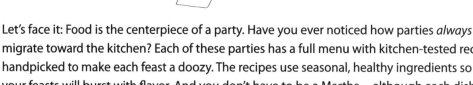

Let's face it: Food is the centerpiece of a party. Have you ever noticed how parties *always* migrate toward the kitchen? Each of these parties has a full menu with kitchen-tested recipes handpicked to make each feast a doozy. The recipes use seasonal, healthy ingredients so that your feasts will burst with flavor. And you don't have to be a Martha—although each dish is beautiful to look at and delicious to eat, the recipes are suited for a beginning cook. You don't have to be a Trump either—the ingredients are easy to find and relatively inexpensive (no snails stuffed with caviar here). Generally, the recipes are for eight. You can cut them in half for a more intimate group of four, or multiply them for a big shebang.

Adding Pizzazz

Your guests' experience begins the second they knock on your door. Each chapter is packed with ideas to tickle every single one of your guests' senses through simple, creative decorating ideas. It's the little touches that your friends will remember. And if you want to go *all* the way, there are also ideas for favors (and even costumes) for you and your guests.

Bring in the Entertainment! ::::::::::::::::::::

Here's where this book takes your parties one step further than the average party book. Parties aren't just about canapés and centerpieces—there's a reason we celebrate! Some of these activities are just for fun, and some are to bring your friendships to a deeper level and get you and your guests thinking about important spiritual truths.

I know what you're thinking: "Oh no! Here come the awkward, churchy games, and I'd rather eat rotten sushi than do them with my friends." Relax, the activities included are bona fide non-cheesy. (Well, OK, *most* of the time they're not cheesy.) No "if you were a fruit, what kind of fruit would you be" questions. These activity ideas are fun ways to get to know one another better and to rejoice in God and in your friendships.

Book Club :::::::::::::::::::::

Looking for a way to shake up your book club? For each month, I'll give you ideas for books that relate to the theme. You can adapt each party to be a theme dinner for your book club. I'm *not* necessarily endorsing the entire content of all the books, so read at your own risk.

There's one last ingredient to throwing a fabulous party—the most important one!
Before (and during) your party, be praying that God would use it to draw women toward him, to strengthen friendships, and to glorify him!

So are you ready to get partying? Grab a spatula and some friends, and in a year's time, you're going to be some serious *party divas!*

Spring

"Always a Bridesmaid" Brunch

• Perfect for large-group spring event

There's just something in the spring air that kicks a particular female gene into gear. It makes us ladies inexplicably yearn to dress up fancy and eat fussy foods with our pinkies in the air. Spring reminds us of so many years past—of our first prom, our best friend's shower, our daughter's wedding. Get together with your friends to celebrate this season of newness and remember old joys.

This is the kind of event that would be a blast with a bigger group of women. It'd also be a fun event for women to invite their friends from outside of church to.

Menu ::::::::::::::::::

Your elegant brunch will combine all the fresh flavors of spring: asparagus, strawberries, mushrooms, and rhubarb. The dishes are all gorgeous, too, so your girlfriends will feel extra pampered.

Party Tip

Buy thick stalks of asparagus, which will take a little longer to roast. This will ensure your bacon and asparagus are finished cooking at the same time.

Roasted Asparagus Bundles With Maple Dijon Cream Sauce

Enjoy the spring asparagus with this surprising combination of flavors that's perfect for a brunch.

- 1 bunch asparagus (about 1 pound)
- 8 slices maple-flavored bacon
- olive oil
- 1 cup whipping cream
- ⅓ cup maple syrup
- 1 tablespoon Dijon mustard
- ⅛ teaspoon nutmeg
- salt and pepper

Preheat oven to 400 degrees. Wash asparagus and break off woody ends. Set on baking sheet, drizzle with a very small amount of olive oil, and sprinkle with salt and pepper. Toss to coat.

Divide asparagus into 8 bundles. Tie a slice of bacon around the center of each bundle. Let ends of bacon drape to the sides. Arrange evenly on baking sheet. Bake in oven for 12 to 15 minutes, until bacon is done.

Meanwhile, combine whipping cream and syrup in a small saucepan over medium heat. Simmer for 12 to 15 minutes, until slightly thickened. Add mustard, nutmeg, and salt to taste. Simmer another minute. Drizzle sauce over bundles and serve immediately. Serves 8.

Wild Mushroom Quiche

Mmm…This quiche is so decadently delicious, it will make your brunch a special occasion.

- ○ 3 tablespoons butter
- ○ ½ cup chopped yellow onion
- ○ ½ pound mushrooms, wiped clean and sliced (Any kind you please—I prefer all cremini)
- ○ 1 large clove garlic, minced
- ○ ½ teaspoon dried thyme
- ○ ½ teaspoon dry mustard
- ○ ½ teaspoon salt
- ○ ¼ teaspoon pepper
- ○ 3 large eggs
- ○ 1 cup whipping cream
- ○ 1 cup shredded jack cheese
- ○ 1 store-bought deep dish pie crust, thawed
- ○ 3 ounces freshly grated Parmesan cheese

Preheat oven to 350 degrees. Prick holes in thawed pie crust with a fork, and bake for five minutes. In a large skillet, melt butter over medium-high heat. Add onions and cook for three minutes, occasionally stirring. Add the mushrooms and cook about five minutes more. Add garlic and cook an additional minute. Add thyme and mustard, and season with salt and pepper. Remove from heat and let cool.

Beat eggs and combine with cream. Add salt, pepper, and jack cheese. Place the vegetable mixture in the crust. Pour in egg mixture and top with Parmesan. Bake for 30-35 minutes, until set. Remove from oven and let cool for 30 minutes before serving. Serves 6-8.

Party Tip

This quiche will make eight cute little petite servings. But, trust me, it's so divine, you might want to plan on one quiche per six women.

Party Tip

Not all pie crusts are equal. If the crust you buy is in a shallow tin, carefully transfer the crust to a deeper pie plate to bake in. Are you a baking diva? Then, by all means, make a homemade crust!

Chilled Cantaloupe Soup

This soup makes for an eye-catching display of color garnished with strawberries. The mild flavor complements the wild mushroom quiche just right.

- ○ 2 cantaloupes cut in chunks
- ○ ¼ cup orange juice concentrate
- ○ juice of 1 lime
- ○ 2 tablespoons fresh mint
- ○ 1 tablespoon honey
- ○ 2 cups nonfat vanilla yogurt
- ○ salt
- ○ strawberries and mint sprigs for garnish

Combine the cantaloupe, orange juice concentrate, lime juice, mint, and honey in a food processor. Blend until soup reaches a smooth consistency. If your food processor is small, blend soup in batches. Transfer to a bowl and stir in yogurt. If your cantaloupe is mild, add a pinch of salt to bring out the flavor. Can be made a day in advance.

Serve in shallow bowls garnished with a mint spring in the middle of each. Surround the mint by five strawberry slices, tips pointing in, to look like a flower. Serves 8.

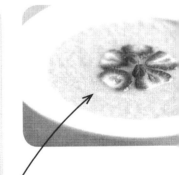

Rhubarb Strawberry Cooler

This frothy, refreshing cooler would be a nice way to start your party.

- 1¼ pounds rhubarb, cut into ½-inch pieces
- 1¼ cups sugar
- 7 cups water
- 3½ cups frozen strawberries

Bring rhubarb, sugar, and water to boil in a large pot; simmer for 15 minutes, stirring occasionally. (The rhubarb will begin to disintegrate.) Cool for 15 minutes. Pour through a fine sieve into a pitcher, pressing hard on the rhubarb solids. (Discard solids.) Chill for several hours until cool. Can be made the day before your party.

Just before serving, whirl juice with frozen strawberries in blender or food processor in batches until frothy. Serve immediately. Serves 8. If you like your rhubarb strong, use fewer strawberries.

Strawberry Phyllo Cups

Prepare to impress: These desserts are stunners! And don't be intimidated by the phyllo dough—it looks tricky at first, but it's really quite simple to use.

- 12 sheets phyllo dough
- ¼ cup melted butter
- 1 cup part-skim ricotta
- 4 ounces light cream cheese, softened
- 3 tablespoons powdered sugar
- ½ teaspoon vanilla
- zest of one lemon
- 1 pound strawberries, sliced

Heat oven to 350. Thaw phyllo dough in fridge overnight (or per package directions). Once thawed, unroll and cover with plastic wrap and then a damp towel. Keep dough covered when you're not using it, as it will dry out. Place one sheet of dough on a baking sheet and brush lightly with melted butter. Layer 3 more sheets, brushing each with butter. Using kitchen scissors, cut into 4-inch squares. Press squares into a muffin pan, forming cups. Continue until all sheets are used. Bake for 5 minutes, until cups are golden, and let cool. (These can be made several days ahead of time and stored in a dry place in an airtight container.)

For the filling: Mix together the cream cheese, ricotta, sugar, vanilla, and lemon zest. Chill until use. Sprinkle strawberries with sugar, if desired. Just before serving, assemble by spooning a tablespoon or so filling into each cup and arranging several strawberry slices on top. Makes approximately 24 cups.

Adding Pizzazz

- **The first element to your pizzazz** is easy—it's all about the dresses! Who hasn't dropped 100 clams on some gown only to be worn once and then shoved into the netherworld of the wardrobe? Ask women to come in their favorite, their most atrocious, their fussiest, and their most jaw-dropping of dresses. The demographics of your guests will determine the drift of your party. Mainly young adults? Maybe prom-themed is the way to go. Mainly middle-aged? Pull out the wedding garb. Prime-timers? Pick an era!

- **Buy several disposable cameras** to set on your table or tables (like those left on tables at wedding receptions). Encourage women to be creative while taking pictures of one another, the meal, and the games. You can share the pictures with your friends after the party.

- **Choose a mix of your favorite high-school dance or romance songs** to play during the brunch. Before the party, you could ask women the theme songs from their proms, their "first dance" songs from their weddings, or their favorite love songs. Then gather those songs to play at the party. As it's an elegant meal, you could also simply play classical music or music from the '30s and '40s, such as Nat King Cole and Frank Sinatra.

- **Flowers are a great way to decorate for spring.** Place fresh-picked flowers around your area, such as hydrangea, tulips, or daffodils. Small budget and no garden? Wildflowers and, yes, even dandelions can look pretty when cleaned and tied in bunches with brightly colored ribbon.

- **A fantastic surprise for the water glasses is flower petal ice cubes.** Simply wash flower petals, place them in an ice cube tray, fill with water, and freeze. Here are some popular edible flowers you can get at the store or in your own yard (buy organic and make sure no pesticides have been used on them): apple blossoms, carnation petals, chrysanthemums, Johnny-jump-ups, lavender, lilacs, pansies, roses, and violets. Here are some toxic flowers to steer clear of: azaleas, daffodils, daisies, delphiniums, hyacinths, morning glories, orchids, petunias, and sweet peas.

- **For party favors or decorations, make candied rose petals and cream cheese wedding mints.** Both recipes are really simple and will add such a nice touch. You can bundle up a few mints for each woman in tulle circles (found at craft stores) tied with ribbon for favors. Or place the mints on plates around your party area.

- **You can place the candied rose petals** around the edge of each mint plate or scatter them on your dining table as part of the setting. The petals would also be lovely as a garnish for the dessert plates. (And, yes, you can eat the rose petals, but use your own discretion about eating raw egg whites.)

Party Tip

Suggest thrift storin' it for vintage garb if you think women might worry about fitting into their old dresses.

Party Tip

This party is about celebrating the seasons of life—all of them! If you have many single, widowed, or divorced guests, be extra sensitive of the little comments dropped at the party. You might even want to just go with a formal-gown party so they don't get asked over and over, "So why didn't *you* wear your wedding dress?"

Spring

Candied Rose Petals

- ○ petals from one or two organic roses
- ○ 2 egg whites
- ○ 1 cup of sugar

Wash the rose petals, and pat dry. Use a pastry brush to brush each petal with egg whites. Place each petal in the sugar and use a spoon to coat with sugar. Let rose petals sit out on a baking sheet overnight.

Cream Cheese Wedding Mints

- ○ 4 ounces cream cheese, softened
- ○ 2½ cups powdered sugar
- ○ ¼ teaspoon peppermint extract
- ○ food coloring
- ○ granulated sugar

Mix first four ingredients together using an electric beater until well-blended. If you like, make several colors of mints, or use lemon extract in place of peppermint extract. Roll mixture into small balls, and roll in granulated sugar. Set on wax paper. Use your pinky finger to press down the middle of each ball. If you have rubber molds, you can press the mints into these. Makes approximately 10 dozen mints.

Party Tip

These mints can be frozen for several months and are an easy way to prepare ahead of time for your party. It's a good idea to freeze them before your party so that they'll stay cold longer when set out. (They thaw quickly.)

- **For table decoration,** fill clear glass fishbowls with water, add one drop of blue food coloring, and float flowers or floating candles in the bowls.
- **Another easy way to create a spring look is with fruit.** Place lemons, oranges, and limes in large, clear fruit bowls or hurricane glasses, and place them around your party area.
- **If you're trying to keep decorations low-budget,** use colored card stock to create daisy decorations. Even the most artistically challenged can draw the outline of a five-petal daisy. Cut out 6-inch daisy outlines and glue colored circles in the middle. Punch a hole in the top of one of the petals, loop ribbon through the holes, and hang them from the ceiling. If you can handle more than just a daisy outline, use card stock to make butterfly cutouts, too.
- **To go all out,** create floral pomanders using craft foam balls, fresh flower buds, and ribbon to hang from the ceiling or your door. You could even create mini-pomanders to place at each woman's place setting as a favor.

Bring in the Entertainment!

A lot of the fun of your party will just happen naturally—women oohing and aahing over their dresses and dishing about where they came from. Make sure everyone tells the stories of the dresses during the meal. (For example, I would tell a little story about why I own not one, but two of the same brown bridesmaid dress: A month before the wedding, I nearly set the dress on fire by hanging it in front of a radiator. The dress turned an odd yellowish blue, and a new dress had to be ordered.)

Most Horrid Bridesmaid Dress Ever Contest

So far, I've been a bridesmaid *seven* times. That's at least $700 worth of fabric getting nibbled by happy little moths right now ($800 with the second brown dress)! And trust me, the dresses weren't all worth it. But maybe it would be some compensation if I had the honor of winning The Most Horrid Bridesmaid Dress Ever Contest. Wouldn't *you* feel better?

Have fun with contest categories: **"Most Likely to Have Appeared on *Dallas*," "Puffiest Sleeves," "Color Most Likely to Make Babies Cry,"** or **"Dress Most Worthy of Being Set on Fire and Stomped On."** You can make the contest simple: Before or after the meal, have women stand to nominate themselves. Then use rounds of applause to determine the winners. Or, as women arrive at your party, have slips of paper for them to check off which categories they'd like to be considered for. Prepare ballots beforehand. Pass out the ballots, let women know which dresses are nominated, and have women anonymously fill the ballots out during your party. This would be a good place to throw in some nice categories, too, such as "Most Elegant," "Most Likely to Woo Humphrey Bogart," "Most Marilyn-esque" or "Most Classic."

At the end of your party, announce the winners. Make fun award certificates, or bring on the prizes! These, too, can be silly. Most Worthy of Being Set on Fire and Stomped On? Award a box of matches. Most Likely to Have Appeared on *Dallas*? A "Don't Mess With Texas" bumper sticker. Most Marilyn-esque? A tube of red lipstick. Whatever you do, make sure it's fun!

The Ultimate Cheesy Shower Game

Don't worry, you don't have to create a wedding dress out of a roll of toilet paper. And you don't have to do some lame "unscramble the wedding words" game. And you don't have to be fastest to put on four items from your honeymoon suitcase. No, you don't have to do any one of those cheesy shower games. You have to do all three of them at the same time! That's right, three of the most dreaded cheesy shower games of all time, all rolled into one relay.

Party Tip

Here's the important part: Make sure women actually nominate their own dresses. How dreadful if Milly came in her best old musty dress, pleased as punch with her high fashion, only to be given the honor of "Most Horrid" dress! If you decide to do the contest, make sure you let women know when you invite them.

Also very important: Chances are *some* of the brides who chose the horrid dresses will be in attendance at your party (that is, if your friends are still on speaking terms after wearing the dresses in question). It might be a good idea to disqualify any contestant from the competition whose dress is from another person's wedding in the room, or your party might come to blows.

Spring

Party Tip

The dress women construct must stay on for the entirety of the game. (To qualify, the dress must pass the test of "wouldn't get the wearer arrested for indecent exposure if worn outside.")

Party Tip

Choose the questions that are most appropriate for the demographics of your guests!

If you're in a large group, form teams. If not, have your friends get in pairs. Each team will have two minutes to create a wedding dress using one roll of toilet paper.

After two minutes, teams will rush to a suitcase at the other end of the room. The partner not wearing the paper dress must put on all four honeymoon-clothing items in the case on top of her clothes with her partner's help. (A bikini top, a snorkel mask, a sun hat, and a Hawaiian shirt would work well. Make sure the clothes will fit everyone invited.)

As soon as this partner is dressed, the teams will rush to the other end of the room (taking care not to rip that fragile paper dress) to complete the "Wedding Word Scramble" you've prepared. (Have three scrambled wedding-theme words written on each paper. ("Rebid," "lebls," and "nirg" would work well for "bride," "bells," and "ring.") Or make it a little harder: "nelomiusi" for "limousine," "pireceont" for "reception," and "sutoaruse" for "trousseau." The first team or pair to successfully unscramble the three words, with the honeymoon attire and paper dress intact, wins!

This game will be especially difficult with women in their fancy attire, so make sure they're careful in those heels! Some ideas for the prizes: a toy wedding-tiara, candy rings or necklaces, or dollar gift certificates to an ice-cream shop.

Gab Time

If you want to get into some good conversations during your party, here's a list of questions you can discuss during the meal. Or type them up and place at each table if you're having a large gathering.

- What's your favorite or most embarrassing school dance story?
- What is it about dances that sometimes gets us chicks so giddy?
- Often, dances are all about the makeup and the hair and the dress. (We spend more time on our makeup than actually dancing!) Where do you think this impulse to primp comes from?
- Is this an OK thing? a bad thing? a good thing?
- How can you have a healthy, balanced attitude toward getting gussied up while still having a good time?
- When you were a girl, did you dream about what your wedding would be like (or were you busy climbing trees)?
- If so, what was your dream wedding like?
- Tell your best or worst bridesmaid experience.
- If you're married, what was your favorite part of your wedding?
- As Christians, we're called the bride of Christ. Why do you think that particular comparison was made rather than "the child" or "the business partner" of Christ?
- What can you do each day to remember that you're Christ's bride (and act like it!)?

Speaking Topic Ideas

If you want to use this celebration as a church-wide women's event, you might also want to have a speaker give a short talk. Here are some ideas for topics:

- We are the bride of Christ. (Matthew 9:15)

- What is true beauty? (Proverbs 31; 1 Peter 3:3-5)

- As spring promises renewal, God promises to renew us. (2 Corinthians 5:17-18; Colossians 3:9-10)

Book Club :::::::::::::::::::::

Till We Have Faces by C.S. Lewis. A retelling of the myth of Psyche, a metaphor for our marriage with Christ. Beautiful writing and a different side of Lewis.

Traveling Mercies: Some Thoughts on Faith by Anne Lamott. The author's rich, if reluctant, travels toward God.

Spring

I Love Paris in the Springtime

- A great party to invite new friends to

- Good for a small group of friends

Ah, "gay Paris." (Read that in your best French accent.) The smell of pastries wafting down the wandering, cobblestone streets. Little poodles riding in the wire baskets of bicycles. Mimes on street corners…

OK, I'm gonna level with you: I've never been to Paris. But I've always felt a kinship with the place thanks to our shared passion: food. Gastronomy is paramount in Paris. So even if you're in Kentucky and think, like me, that Paris is filled with poodles and mimes, you can still have the heartbeat of the Parisian lifestyle as you sit down to a simple, delicious meal made from the finest of ingredients. Make the cheese-tasting the crown of your party if you wish, or keep it simple. This party is best for a pleasant, relaxed afternoon or evening with friends. It's outreach friendly, so invite whatever friends you wish without worrying about making them uncomfortable.

Party Tip ✳

French onion soups usually use Gruyère, Swiss, or Jarlsberg cheese. I prefer the milder Mozzarella that is much easier on the wallet.

Menu

Serve your French meal in courses so guests can fully savor and enjoy each course. Start with the soup, followed by the scallops. Serve the simple green salad *after* the scallops, to cleanse the palate. In France, the salad comes after the entrée, and the cheese course always comes before dessert. Note that these recipes each serve 4 to 6 people for a smaller party. If you were at my party, I'd make you all speak in French accents during the whole meal. But, then again, you and your friends might be a bit more *en vogue* than I.

Really French Onion Soup

The nutmeg and thyme in this soup imbue it with a subtle, more traditional French flavor, setting it apart from the Americanized French Onion Soups you find at many American restaurants.

- 1½ pounds yellow onions, about 3 medium
- 2 tablespoons butter
- ½ teaspoon sugar
- 4 cups beef stock
- ½ cup red wine
- 1 bay leaf
- ¼ teaspoon thyme
- ¼ teaspoon freshly ground nutmeg
- salt to taste
- 1 tablespoon flour
- ¼ cup freshly grated Parmesan cheese
- ½ cup Mozzarella cheese ✳ *(see margin note)*
- 4-6 slices of French baguette, toasted

Peel and thinly slice onions. In a large pot, melt butter. Add onions and cook on medium-low for 30 minutes, until lightly browned. Add sugar halfway into cooking time to caramelize onions. In the meantime, in a medium saucepan, heat stock and add wine, bay leaf, thyme, and nutmeg. Simmer while onions cook.

After onions have cooked, lightly season with salt. Add flour and cook, stirring, for 1 minute. Then add the stock mixture from the saucepan to the pot with onions, and bring to a simmer. Simmer covered for 25 minutes. (If you have time, the longer you simmer, the richer the soup.) Add Parmesan cheese and simmer 5 minutes more. Divide into ovenproof bowls, and top each serving with a toasted baguette slice and sprinkle with the Mozzarella cheese. Broil for several minutes, until cheese is bubbly. Serve hot. Makes 4 to 6 servings.

Party Tip

If you don't have ovenproof bowls, place the baguette slices on a baking sheet and sprinkle with the cheese. Broil these for several minutes until the cheese is bubbly, then place on top of each soup bowl.

Lemon Tarragon Scallops

Many people think of French food as fussy and hard to make, but it just isn't so. This easy recipe highlights the simplicity of good Parisian food. The scallops cook quickly, so sauté them after your guests have finished the soup.

- 1½ pounds sea scallops
- ½ teaspoon salt
- ¼ teaspoon freshly ground black pepper
- flour (just enough to coat scallops)
- 1 tablespoon olive oil
- 3 tablespoon butter
- 2 large shallots, minced
- 1 clove garlic, minced
- 1 tablespoon fresh tarragon, chopped
- ¼ cup dry white wine
- 1 tablespoon lemon juice

Slice scallops in half horizontally. Toss with flour, salt, and pepper. Heat oil and 2 tablespoons butter in a large skillet over medium-high heat until sizzling. Add scallops and brown for 2 minutes without moving them. Turn and sauté for 2 more minutes.

Add the remaining tablespoon of butter, along with the shallots and garlic, and sauté for 30 seconds. Add the wine, lemon juice, and tarragon, and sauté for another 1 minute. Serve immediately, pouring sauce over scallops. Makes 4 to 6 servings.

Party Tip

To save time, you can slice the scallops before the party and toss them with the flour, salt, and pepper.

Party Tip

I'd serve the scallops alone, but you can serve with a side of white rice or couscous if you wish.

Spring

Simple Green Salad

Sometimes simple is best.

- ○ 2 heads bibb or butter lettuce
- ○ 1 clove garlic, minced
- ○ 1 shallot, minced
- ○ 3 tablespoons olive oil
- ○ 2 tablespoons white wine vinegar
- ○ 1 tablespoon fresh tarragon, chopped
- ○ ½ teaspoon coarse sea salt
- ○ freshly ground black pepper

Wash and dry lettuce and place in a large bowl in refrigerator until ready to serve. Place garlic, shallot, and oil in a small bowl and let sit for 15 to 45 minutes. Immediately before serving, beat the vinegar into the oil and add tarragon. Pour over salad and toss, seasoning with salt and pepper. (You may wish to serve the dressing on the side so each can add how much she wishes—the dressing has a strong tarragon flavor.) Makes 4 to 6 servings.

Party Tip

Toss fruit slices with lemon juice to prevent discoloration.

Party Tip

If there's a good bakery in your area, for an easy end to your meal, buy some good French pastries or a fruit tart.

Cheese Platter for Cheese Tasting

Here are some ideas for what to serve on your cheese platter. Thorough instructions for cheese-tasting protocol are given in the "Bring in the Entertainment" section.

- ○ fruit slices, such as pear and apple
- ○ bread rounds or crackers
- ○ brie (a mild, soft cow's whole-milk cheese)
- ○ Port du Salut (an elastic cheese similar in taste to Gouda)
- ○ Boursin (a cow's-milk triple-cream cheese, available coated with herbs or peppers)
- ○ Cantal (a hard, yellow cheese with a piquant flavor)
- ○ Roquefort (a blue-veined cheese with a sharp, peppery flavor)

Crème Brûlée

I've eaten a lot of crème brûlée in my life, but I've yet to find one to rival my mother-in-law's. Here's the secret recipe, courtesy of Nancy Van Schooneveld.

- ○ 6 egg yolks
- ○ ½ cup sugar (extra fine if you can find it)
- ○ 1 teaspoon cornstarch dissolved in 2 teaspoons milk
- ○ 3 cups heavy whipping cream, scalded
- ○ 1 teaspoon vanilla
- ○ light brown sugar

Beat egg yolks with sugar in the top pan of a double boiler until very thick. Blend in the cornstarch dissolved in milk. Gradually stir in the heated cream. Cook over simmering water and stir constantly until it thickens. The maximum temperature should be about 170 degrees on an instant-read thermometer. Remove from heat and add vanilla. Pour into 6 individual heat-proof ramekins. Cool; then chill until surface is firm.

You can prepare the crème brûlée to this point up to 2 days before serving.

Sift brown sugar about ⅛ inch thick over the top of ramekins. Melt sugar with a small torch. If you don't have a torch, put on cookie sheet and put under the broiler. Watch and turn often until sugar caramelizes. Let cool at room temperature. Serves 6.

Party Tip

Don't add the sugar topping until a few hours before serving so it doesn't soften from the moisture.

Adding Pizzazz

- **Give your party that certain *je ne sais quoi*.** It's not hard to find French decorations. At many craft stores, and even at stores such as Target, you'll find oodles of Parisian décor. Look for Eiffel Tower–themed posters and knickknacks or *Le Chat Noir* posters. Even French café signs are easy to find.

- **Hang dried lavender bunches** or other dried herbs from your ceiling in the kitchen.

- **Shop flea markets for a retro bicycle** with a wire basket, and place it in your party area. Put a bouquet of tulips and a baguette in the basket.

- **If you don't have a bike with a wire basket, place a baguette,** a bottle of sparkling cider, and a bouquet of tulips peeking out of a brown shopping bag on a counter, for a seemingly serendipitous decoration.

- **If you can, use small, round wrought-iron patio tables** or two for your seating to make your party look like a little sidewalk café. Use taper candles and wine glasses for added sophistication.

- **Make signs to use as posters.** Try black construction paper, white paint, and phrases such as *Café Le Paris* or *Gâteau au Chocolat 1 Franc*. Festoon the signs with fleur de lis.

- **Black should be your main décor color, with splashes of red.** A large, black wrought-iron wall clock could be the perfect focal point for the room.

- **Anything with a poodle would work as a decoration.** Especially if it's a pink poodle.

- **To look French chic yourself,** wear a scarf knotted around your neck.

- **Your meal will create sumptuous scents,** but if you want to have candles lit, use lavender- or lemon verbena–scented candles.

- **It's not too hard to get your hands on good French music** to play in the background. How about Celine Dion? Or try movie soundtracks, such as *Something's Gotta Give* or *French Kiss*.

Party Tip

Ooh la la. Ask your friends to come dressed très chic, Parisian style or haute couture.

Bring in the Entertainment!

Cheese Tasting

You can have a simple cheese course during your dinner where guests nibble at the cheeses, or you can take a little more time for a true cheese tasting. Here are tips on how to turn your cheese course into a tasting.

First, choose your cheeses. You'll want to serve three to five kinds of cheese, depending on appetite, time, and budget. You can opt to serve all French cheeses (as listed in the menu section), or buy cheeses according to type (such as blue or goat or mild or semi-soft), or you can buy a wide range of cheeses according to your own taste.

Serve the cheeses at room temperature—set them out about an hour before serving. Label each cheese, and have a different knife to cut each. Give each guest a pen and pad of paper to record her findings. If you serve a beverage, make sure it won't compete with the cheese—water works nicely.

Here's a basic protocol for your tasting: Have guests experience one cheese at a time. Start with the mildest, moving up to the strongest as you progress through the cheeses. Before tasting the cheese, guests can discuss the cheese and jot down their reactions to it. Here are some things to look for: Is the exterior of the cheese crinkly or smooth? What color is it? Does it look oily or dry? Have guests also pay attention to the feel of the cheese—is it soft, firm, or hard? And what does it smell like—earthy, fruity, or pungent?

Now for the tasting. Have guests first taste the cheese without bread or any accompaniment, and note their reactions to it. What does it taste like? Do you like it? After the first taste, have guests sample the cheese with bread or fruit, noting whether it enhances or detracts from the flavor. Move through all of the cheeses in this manner. Encourage guests to describe the cheeses however they see fit, but here are some adjectives commonly used to get your ideas rolling: *acrid, aged, barnyard, clean, creamy, earthy, fishy, fruity, gamy, grainy, moldy, nutty, piquant, pungent, robust, sour, tangy,* and *velvety*.

After your tasting, wait a little bit before serving the dessert so your guests can work up an appetite.

French Lessons

No matter what you say in French, it sounds beautiful. Even the mundane "I'm taking this moldy trash out to the dump" is poetry in the French tongue. Enjoy the lovely melody of the French language together during your French lessons.

Create place cards for each woman. If you're artsy or if you can find pictures, use

Party Tip

If you choose to serve one or two out-of-the-ordinary cheeses, also pick at least one or two mild old favorites, such as Edam or cheddar, so that most guests will know at least one cheese.

pictures of the Eiffel Tower, the Louvre, Montmarte, the Arc de Triomphe, the Notre Dame, and so on as background of one side and write guests' names on that side. On the other side, have fun French sentences. Take turns having each woman attempt to pronounce her sentence and then translate it. (You'll have the translations and can let them know how they do afterward.)

If you wish to take your place card game even further, write a question on the inside of each place card that each woman will then answer. Here are the sentences to write on the cards (Thanks to my French friend Ewy for the translations!):

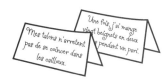

Dans mes rêves les plus fous, je mangerai une paire de cuisse de grenouilles tous les matins. Translation: "In my wildest dreams, I would eat a pair of frog legs every morning." Accompanying question: *Paris is a place of dreams; what is one of your wildest dreams?*

Pour moi, la mode est aussi naturel que la respiration, mais je pense avoir suffoque. Translation: "Fashion is like breathing to me, but I think I might have suffocated." Accompanying question: *How much is fashion worth to you? 1 franc, 20 francs, or 100 francs? or Which magazine describes your fashion: Vogue, Country Living, or Real Simple?*

Mes talons n'arrêtent pas de se coincer dans les cailloux. Translation: "My high heels keep getting stuck in these cobblestones." Accompanying question: *Be honest. How many pairs of shoes do you own?*

Je ne savais pas comment ni pour quoi utiliser mon bidet, alors j'ai planté des violettes dedans. Translation: "I didn't know what my bidet was supposed to be used for, so I planted some violets in it." Accompanying question: *What's the one part of your daily beauty routine you could absolutely not survive without?*

Une fois, j'ai mangé vingt beignets en deux minutes pendant un pari. Translation: "I once ate 20 donuts in two minutes on a dare." Accompanying question: *What food are you most over-the-top crazy about?*

La romance de Paris me donne l'impression d'être une jeune femme à nouveau. Translation: "The romance of the Paris city streets make me feel like a young maiden again." Accompanying question: *What's your idea of true romance?*

Book Club

French Women Don't Get Fat by Mireille Guiliano. One of my favorite books—the author highly recommends cheese, bread, and chocolate to stay trim and happy. My kind of woman!

A Year in Provence by Peter Mayle. The title really says it all.

Party Tip

Have a small prize for the most accurate (or the funniest) translation. Prizes could be high-quality chocolate, a specialty cheese, or French souvenirs found at most craft stores (or even a trip to Paris…just invite me to your party).

Spring

The Feast of Esther

• Fun large-group event

If you've never celebrated this holiday, you're in for a treat. It includes a lot of fun, costumes, food, celebrating, and laughing. The Feast of Esther, also called Purim, is a Jewish holiday that occurs in March each year and celebrates how God saved the Jews from genocide during the reign of King Xerxes in Persia. Queen Esther was married to Xerxes. When he gave the go-ahead to annihilate the Jewish race, Esther risked her own life, spoke up for her people, and saved the Jews. Besides having such rich and meaningful history, Purim is one of the most fun-filled, lighthearted Jewish holidays and is a great event for you to have some fun while remembering how God protects and saves his people.

Menu

There's no one traditional meal served at Purim. Some eat traditional Jewish fare, and others eat a Persian meal to remember Esther's home in Persia. This feast is a combination of the two. Challah bread and hamentaschen are traditional Jewish recipes found at most Purim parties. The other recipes are Persian dishes.

Challah

This sweet Jewish egg bread is a common treat for the Sabbath and Purim. The braids of bread are said to be a reminder of Haman's noose. (You'll read more about Haman later in the chapter.)

- ○ 1¼ cups warm water
- ○ 1½ teaspoons active dry yeast
- ○ ¼ cup honey, plus 1 tablespoon
- ○ 2 tablespoons vegetable oil
- ○ 2 eggs
- ○ ¼ teaspoon almond extract
- ○ 1 teaspoon salt
- ○ 4 cups all-purpose flour

Sprinkle yeast over warm water in a large bowl. Beat in ¼ cup honey, oil, 1 egg, almond extract, and salt. Then add the flour a small amount at a time, beating after each addition. As dough thickens, knead it. Knead until smooth and no longer sticky, adding flour as needed. Cover with a damp towel and let rise until doubled, about 1½ hours.

Turn out dough onto a floured surface and knead for 5 minutes, adding flour as necessary. Divide into thirds and roll each into a long "snake," about 1½ inches in diameter. Pinch the ends of the snakes together, and braid from the middle. Place on a greased baking sheet, cover with a damp towel, and let rise for one hour.

Beat the remaining egg and stir in remaining 1 tablespoon of honey, slightly warmed. Brush over the bread. Bake at 375 degrees for about 25-30 minutes. Cool before serving. Makes one large loaf.

Party Tip

If you're not the baking type (I admit it: I myself am not), buy challah from a local bakery or supermarket. You'll recognize it by its yellow braids. If you'd like, add about ¼ cup of raisins to the dough. You can also sprinkle the top of the bread with cinnamon sugar before baking.

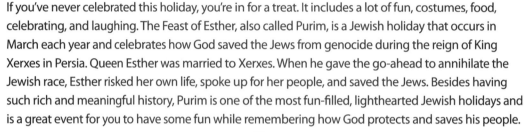

Cucumber Salad

Many Persian meals are accompanied by a simple cucumber mint salad.

- ○ 3 cucumbers, peeled and thinly sliced
- ○ ¾ cup onion, thinly sliced
- ○ 1½ teaspoons salt
- ○ ½ teaspoon black pepper
- ○ 1½ teaspoons dried mint
- ○ 16 ounces plain yogurt
- ○ 5 tablespoons heavy cream

Place sliced cucumbers and onion in a bowl. Combine remaining ingredients and mix well. Pour over cucumbers and toss to coat. Chill several hours before serving. Can be made a day in advance. Serves 8.

Party Tip

If you want to save some calories, use lowfat or fat-free yogurt.

Apricot Chicken With Almond Raisin Rice Pilaf

Apricots, almonds, and raisins are common ingredients in Persian dishes. This is really tasty and really easy. If you want a less sweet dish, use ¾ cup apricot preserves.

- ○ 1½ tablespoons olive oil
- ○ 2 pounds boneless, skinless chicken breasts in ½-inch pieces
- ○ 2 teaspoons paprika
- ○ 1 teaspoon cinnamon
- ○ 2 pinches cardamom
- ○ ½ teaspoon cumin
- ○ ½ teaspoon ginger
- ○ ½ teaspoon salt
- ○ 1 large onion, chopped
- ○ 1 large clove garlic, minced
- ○ ²/₃ cup dried apricots, cut in quarters
- ○ 1 cup apricot preserves
- ○ two 6¼-ounce packages rice pilaf mix
- ○ 4 cups reduced sodium chicken broth
- ○ ²/₃ cup raisins
- ○ 1 cup slivered almonds

Mix paprika, cinnamon, cardamom, cumin, ginger, and salt in a bowl and add cubed chicken, tossing to coat. In very large skillet, heat olive oil over medium heat. Add chicken and onion; sauté 7 to 10 minutes or until chicken is cooked. Add garlic, apricots, and apricot preserves the last 2 minutes of cooking and stir. Keep warm.

In the meantime, prepare pilaf according to package directions, substituting chicken broth for water and adding raisins. Serve chicken over rice and sprinkle with almonds. Makes 8 servings.

Bread, Cheese, and Herb Plate

At most Persian meals, there will be a plate of fresh veggies, cheeses, and bread to pass around the table. Traditionally, you would grab a piece of bread, spread it with some cheese, and top it with a vegetable and some herbs. Here's a list of some ideas for your plate.

- flat bread
- pita wedges
- radishes, halved
- cucumber rounds

- feta cheese
- bunches of fresh herbs, such as mint, parsley, basil, and tarragon

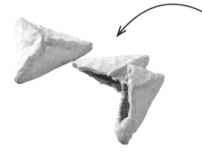

✳ Hamantaschen

These traditional Purim cookies are said to look like Haman's tri-cornered hat (or maybe even his ears!). These are commonly given as gifts to friends or neighbors on Purim.

- 1½ cups butter, softened
- 1 cup sugar
- 2 eggs
- 1 teaspoon almond extract
- 6 tablespoons orange juice

- 1 tablespoon vanilla
- 2 teaspoons baking powder
- 4½ cups flour
- jam (whatever flavor you like)

Cream butter and sugar in a large mixing bowl. Beat the eggs in 1 at a time. Mix in almond, vanilla, and orange juice. Gradually mix in flour and baking powder until dough forms a ball. Cover and refrigerate for several hours or overnight.

On a floured surface, roll dough out to ¼-inch thickness. Cut into 3-inch circles using a round cookie cutter or the rim of a glass. Place 1 teaspoon of jam in the center of each cookie. Fold in three sides to form a triangle, overlapping in the middle so only a small amount of jam shows. Bake on a greased cookie sheet for 10 to 12 minutes at 375 degrees. Can be made several days in advance. Makes about 4 dozen cookies.

Adding Pizzazz ⋯⋯⋯⋯⋯⋯

Here's a bit of trivia for you: One of the "mitzvahs" (requirements) of Purim is that one drinks enough wine so that he can't tell the difference between the phrases "blessed be Mordecai" and "cursed be Haman." I'm not recommending that you intoxicate your friends, but this at least gives you an idea of the kind of celebration Purim is—it's fun, joyous, and a little wild! Really have fun celebrating how much God loves his people. From the second your guests arrive, let them know that this is a party!

Party Tip

If you'd like a drink to serve before the feast or on the side, go with pomegranate juice. It looks dazzling in a glass and is quite healthy. Serve with a splash of club soda.

- **Have upbeat party music playing throughout the night.** If you can find Jewish celebration music, great. If not, play some of your own party favorites. Think "Dancing in the Streets," "Celebration," and "We Are Family."

- **This party is super easy to decorate for:** Just think outrageous birthday party. Raid your local party store, and stock up on some essentials. Use multicolored paper plates, napkins, and cups. Spread confetti on the tables.

- **Have crayons at each table for guests to doodle** with during the meal. Use brightly colored butcher paper as tablecloths. Have noisemakers on the tables, too, for your Esther melodrama.

- **Decorate with rich bursts of color**—go with jewel tones, such as emerald, amethyst, and ruby red, to play up a royal Persian atmosphere.

- **Drape the ceilings with brightly colored sheets for a Persian feel.** If you have some fun, bright pillows, spread them in groups on the floor for women to lounge on while chatting with one another, Persian style.

Party Tip

Your attitude will set the mood for the party—the focus should be on a fun celebration, not on how perfect your food or setting are. Have a smile on your face and be ready to celebrate!

Bring in the Entertainment!

There are several traditions that every Purim celebration has gotta have.

Costume Contest

Did you know there's a Jewish holiday in which men dress up as women and have a beauty contest? Yep, it's Purim. The Jews consider Purim to be a hidden miracle, God's hidden providence in saving them. That's part of the symbolism of the Hamantaschen cookies—they look plain on the outside, but they have a tasty filling on the inside. So children and adults also dress up to symbolize the hidden miracle. Stage your own Purim costume contest. No, you don't have to have a cross-dressing beauty contest, just a fun costume contest. Pick a theme for women to dress up as, such as movie characters or famous queens, or let women come up with their own costume ideas.

The Melodramatic Megillah

The Megillah, or the Book of Esther, is always read out loud on Purim. Traditionally, children have noisemakers they sound when Haman's name is said, and they cheer when Esther's or Mordecai's name is said. You can read Esther after the meal, while everyone is digesting. Encourage your guests to cheer when you read about Esther or Mordecai, and boo and hiss when you read about Haman. Pass out party horns or noisemakers for them to use, too. You could even perform your very own melodrama, if you have some theatric types among your friends. (Oftentimes melodramas with actors portraying Haman, King Xerxes, Esther, and Mordecai are performed for children on Purim.) If you want, you can shorten the reading a bit, too, reading just the major plot points of the story.

Spring

Party Tip

On Purim, it's more important to remember the poor than to have a magnificent spread. So if you're trying to decide between those fancy party balloons and a gift to charity, go with the latter.

Party Tip

This is a great opportunity for you and your friends to experience the disciplines of prayer and fasting together if you never have before.

Alms for the Poor

Another important tradition of Purim is to give to the poor. Each person (even children) gives a small amount to someone in need. Tell your guests about this tradition before the party, and set out a donation basket at the party. You can decide together with your guests what charity or person to give the donations to.

Gifts of Friendship

To celebrate God's goodness and express community, people give small gifts of food to their friends on Purim. It might be a small basket of fruit and candied nuts, or a plate of cookies. You could celebrate this by giving each woman who attends a small gift, such as a bag of spiced candied nuts or a plate of hamentaschen. You can also tell your guests about the tradition, and then make cards together at the party for friends. In the next week, everyone can deliver a plate of goodies with a card to someone in order to reach out with God's love.

The Fast of Esther

The day before the feast of Esther, there is a fast to remember how Esther fasted before approaching the king. Ask your friends to fast the day before your celebration and to spend this time in prayer for God's people who are persecuted across the globe. You can find specific needs to pray for at Web sites such as www.persecutedchurch.org. Then you can spend some time praying together at the party if you'd like, too.

Gab Time

If you want to dig a little deeper into the meaning of this holiday, discuss these questions in small groups. You can print them up on a card, and set them at the tables.

- Have you ever experienced a "hidden miracle"? (Something that seemed *really* bad at first, but that God used for good in your life.)

- Esther 4:14 says, "For if you remain silent at this time, relief and deliverance for the Jews will arise from another place, but you and your father's family will perish. And who knows but that you have come to royal position for such a time as this?" Is there a position you've been given that you could use in order to do good?

- If deliverance will arise from another place if we do nothing, why should we bother doing good?

- Esther asked all the Jewish people and her maids to fast and pray with her. Are you bold enough in asking for prayer and help when you need it?

- Esther says, "If I perish, I perish" (Esther 4:16). Have you ever had this attitude regarding a good (but dangerous) task you had to do (Like protecting your children)? Is there a situation in your life in which you should develop more of this kind of attitude?

- God saved the Jews in a very dramatic way, through Esther. What's one way God has saved or protected you?

Book Club

Esther by Charles Swindoll. A retelling of the story of Esther.

The Hiding Place by Corrie ten Boom. A family in the Netherlands saved many Jews from the Nazis by hiding them in their home during World War II.

Summer

Market Day in Tuscany

• Perfect for a couple of friends on an easy summer day
• Little prep necessary
• Great for making or deepening friendships in a small group

When the weather is just warming and the farmer's market is beginning to fill with the scents of summer, the time is right for an impromptu Italian feast with friends. This feast is so easy to prepare that your guests can make it alongside you. If you want to get to know those new neighbors across the street or if you want some quality time with a couple of close friends, plan a relaxing Tuscan afternoon on your patio. You can use these ideas to add zip to your party, but don't be afraid to make it simple. One thing we can learn from the Italians: They savor their time together over a good meal. Time spent at the table is so important to Italians, they refer to their dining table as sacro desco, the sacred table. So, let this menu be your gateway to relishing your sacred friends. Mangiamo!

Party Tip

This is molto importante! Depending on where you live, this feast may be best saved until late summer, if the tomatoes and peaches are ripest then. Your feast is only as good as your produce.

Menu

These recipes capture the bursting flavors of an Italian summer. When produce is at the height of ripeness, you don't have to do much to enhance the flavor (and who wants to work on a summer afternoon anyway?), so these dishes require little work, especially if you ask your friends to help.

Balsamic-Glazed Pearl Onions

This is a great appetizer to prepare in advance and serve at room temperature for guests to snack on.

- ○ one 16-ounce package pearl onions, thawed and drained
- ○ 1 tablespoon olive oil
- ○ ½ cup balsamic vinegar
- ○ ¼ cup beef stock
- ○ 1 tablespoon orange juice

Heat the olive oil in a sauté pan on medium heat and add onions. Saute for 5 minutes. Add remaining ingredients and simmer until onions are tender and glazed, about 15 minutes. Remove onions with a slotted spoon, and reduce remaining sauce on medium heat until thickened. Drizzle over onions. Serve warm or at room temperature. Serves 8.

Party Tip

If you want to feel like a real Italian mama, you can use fresh onions, but don't come blaming me when your fingers are sore from peeling a pound of pearl onions!

Panzanella (Tuscan Bread and Tomato Salad)

Simple but delicious. This quintessential Italian salad will highlight ripe, tasty tomatoes.

- one day-old French baguette (about 18 inches long)
- 5 tablespoons olive oil
- 2 tablespoons balsamic vinegar
- 2 teaspoons salt (coarse sea salt, if possible)
- ¼ teaspoon ground black pepper
- 4 pounds of a variety of ripe tomatoes: cherry tomatoes, heirlooms, or whatever is ripest
- ½ cup basil leaves, cut in strips
- 1 ball fresh mozzarella from the deli (about 4 ounces), sliced

Cut baguette into ½-inch cubes. Chop larger tomatoes into chunks. In a bowl, combine olive oil, vinegar, salt, and pepper. Add tomatoes, bread cubes, basil, and mozzarella, and mix gently. Serve immediately. If you wish to make this ahead of time, mix all ingredients together except for the bread. Add the bread immediately before serving. Serves 8.

Party Tip

To make this extra tasty, toast the bread. Melt 2 tablespoons butter with 2 tablespoons olive oil in a small saucepan over medium heat. Add 1 clove of minced garlic and cook for 1 minute. Cut the bread into cubes, place on a baking sheet and drizzle with the butter mixture. Bake at 350 degrees for 12 to 15 minutes; then let cool before adding to salad.

Prosciutto Wrapped Shrimp

These tasty little shrimp will complement the panzanella perfectly.

- 2 pounds large shrimp, shelled and deveined with tails left on (about 6 shrimp per person)
- 2 tablespoons olive oil
- ¼ cup strips of fresh basil
- 8 ounces prosciutto (dry-cured ham in the specialty section—ask if you can't find it)
- 8 skewers (if using bamboo, soak in water overnight

Preheat broiler or grill on high heat. Cut slices of prosciutto into 1 inch by 3 inch strips. Mix olive oil with basil and brush shrimp with the mixture.

Wrap each shrimp with a piece of prosciutto and thread onto skewers. (If you broil the shrimp, you don't need to use the skewers, just place on the broiler pan.) Grill or broil shrimp for 2 minutes on each side. Serves 8.

Summer

Party Tip

When I served this menu to friends, I was worried it wouldn't be enough food. But between snacking on cheeses and indulging in the mascarpone cream, it made for a bountiful but simple feast. Pair it with lemon water.

Party Tip

If you end up with extra marscapone cream, here's a delicious solution for the bounty: Make sandwich cookies with the amaretti and the marscapone cream. Mmm…

Italian Cheese Platter

For an easy side to the shrimp and Panzanella, serve a platter with a variety of Italian cheeses. You could also throw on some fruit, such as fresh figs or stone fruits, and some bread, such as any bread left over from your baguette. Here are some ideas for cheese to get you started. Go to a cheese shop or specialty food market and talk to the staff to get more ideas.

- fontina (a mild, semisoft, cow's milk cheese with a delicate, nutty flavor)
- pecorino (a sharp, hard cheese made from ewe's milk)
- provolone (a semihard, cow's milk cheese with agreeable flavor)
- parmigiano reggiano (the "king of cheeses," a hard, granular cow's milk cheese)
- taleggio (a cow's milk cheese, refined, mild salty flavor)

Fresh Peaches With Mascarpone Cream and Amaretti

This dessert can be made with whatever fruit is the ripest and sweetest at the time. If the berries are looking better than the stone fruits, create parfaits alternating berries with the cream and cookie crumbles in parfait cups.

- 8 ripe peaches
- 2 cups mascarpone cheese (most grocery stores carry this—if you can't find it, ask!)
- ¼ cup whipping cream
- 1½ tablespoons honey
- 2 teaspoons almond extract
- 16 amaretti cookies (store-bought or recipe follows)

Halve peaches, pit, and set aside. Whisk the marscapone with the cream, honey, and almond extract until it's blended and fluffy. Spoon cheese mixture into peach cavities. Crumble 8 of the cookies and sprinkle them on top of the peaches. Break the other 8 cookies in half and stick a half cookie in the cream of each half peach. Serves 8.

Amaretti

Amaretti are Italian almond cookies that can be found in many grocery stores by the specialty cookies. If you can't find amaretti, almond wafer cookies also work—you can substitute any thin, crispy cookie for them. Or try these!

- 2 cups blanched almonds (with the skins removed)
- ⅔ cup sugar plus 2 tablespoons sugar
- 2 egg whites

Preheat oven to 350 degrees. Spread the almonds on a baking sheet and bake for 2 minutes; then let cool. Decrease oven to 325 degrees. Butter another baking sheet and line it with parchment paper so cookies won't stick. In a food processor, pulse almonds with 2 tablespoons of sugar until almonds are finely chopped. Mix this with ½ cup of sugar.

In a clean mixing bowl, beat egg whites with remaining sugar until stiff peaks form. Fold egg whites into almond mixture. Spoon dough onto baking sheet and bake for 20 minutes at 325 degrees.

Adding Pizzazz

The spirit of this party is to have an easy feast with your friends, so no need to break your back decorating. If you can, have friends meet outside, and let nature do the decorating.

- **Spread a red and white checked tablecloth on your table.**

- **For looks and for aroma,** place several bouquets of basil from the farmer's market in small glasses or vases on your table. They look great, smell great, and your guests can pluck off leaves to season their meal (just remember to wash the herbs first!).

- **Use bright sunflowers as a centerpiece.** To dramatize the yellow, place small attractive lemons in a fruit bowl or hurricane vase.

- **If you don't have a checked tablecloth,** add a bright splash of color by creating a simple table runner. Find a calendar with pictures of Tuscany, and cut the pictures from the mats. Lay the pictures, alternating which direction they face, on self-adhesive paper such as Con-Tact paper. Layer the self-adhesive paper over the top, and trim the excess paper. Place your table runner in the middle of your table for a cheery conversation starter. You could also make place mats this way.

- **If you have your feast at dusk,** use Chianti bottle candles for lighting (or just use them for centerpieces during the day). Simply wash out an old Chianti bottle (the kind that's squat at the bottom and covered with basket-weave). Stick a taper candle into the mouth, and light it so the candle begins to melt down the sides of the bottle.

- **Have your favorite Italian or Italian-inspired music** playing in the background, such as Andrea Bocelli, Cecilia Bartoli, Josh Groban, Il Divo, or the Three Tenors.

- **For unique party gifts your friends are guaranteed to love,** go to **www.pappardellespasta.com**. Pappardelle's is a Denver-based pasta company that makes an incredible variety of dried pastas, such as dark chocolate linguine, basil garlic fettuccine, and saffron red pepper fusilli, for around $6.50 a pound. Order your girlfriends each a special pasta, and print recipes from their Web site for the pastas. These will make pretty little favors on your table.

- **Here's a different way to spice up your table** and have favors for your guests for about $2.50 to $4 each. Buy small, attractive bottles of Italian ingredients, such as pickled garlic, prepared pesto, sun-dried tomatoes, roasted red peppers, capers, artichoke

Party Tip

Stock up on calendars on clearance in January and February. Pictures cut from calendars and slipped into frames make surprisingly sophisticated decorations. Or, if you're like me and never remember to plan ahead, go to www.calendar.com to find calendars of all kinds.

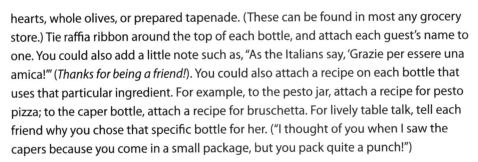

hearts, whole olives, or prepared tapenade. (These can be found in most any grocery store.) Tie raffia ribbon around the top of each bottle, and attach each guest's name to one. You could also add a little note such as, "As the Italians say, 'Grazie per essere una amica!'" (*Thanks for being a friend!*). You could also attach a recipe on each bottle that uses that particular ingredient. For example, to the pesto jar, attach a recipe for pesto pizza; to the caper bottle, attach a recipe for bruschetta. For lively table talk, tell each friend why you chose that specific bottle for her. ("I thought of you when I saw the capers because you come in a small package, but you pack quite a punch!")

- **Another elegant centerpiece and favor are oil bottles.** Buy various shapes and sizes of bottles, and fill them with an assortment of oils (olive, almond, walnut). Spice them up by adding one element to each: For example, fresh chilis in olive oil, citrus peel in walnut oil, and sprigs of herbs in almond oil. Guests can use them as dipping oil if you set any bread out. Then women can each take one home.

Bring in the Entertainment!

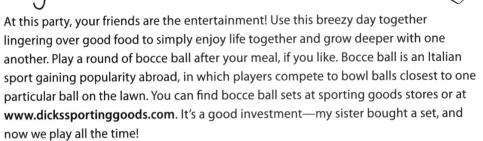

At this party, your friends are the entertainment! Use this breezy day together lingering over good food to simply enjoy life together and grow deeper with one another. Play a round of bocce ball after your meal, if you like. Bocce ball is an Italian sport gaining popularity abroad, in which players compete to bowl balls closest to one particular ball on the lawn. You can find bocce ball sets at sporting goods stores or at **www.dickssportinggoods.com**. It's a good investment—my sister bought a set, and now we play all the time!

If you'd like to extend your *celebrazione* beyond your feast, invite guests inside to watch an "Italian" movie. Here are some great ideas for movies that you'll enjoy and will get you thinking:

- *La Vita è Bella (Life Is Beautiful)* If you watch this movie, chat with your friends afterward about how important humor is in life—especially during the tough times—and how, despite tragedy, life is still beautiful.

- *Enchanted April* If you watch this movie, you'll be inspired to discuss beauty—discovering it in yourselves and in others.

- *Roman Holiday* I don't know if this movie will *actually* get you thinking, but it's got Gregory Peck and Audrey Hepburn—what more could you ask?

If you and your friends are the literary types, spend some time mulling over some great Italian poems and poets. Check out Dante, Petrarca, Boccaccio, and scores more. I'll give you a head start with some ideas here—find the poems at the library or online.

- **"The Canticle of Brother Son"** by St. Francis of Assisi is the first literary work on record written in Italian. Read this poem with one another and discuss the beauty God has created around you. Here are some of the lines:

May Thou be praised, my Lord, with all Thy creatures,
especially mister brother sun,
of whom is the day, and Thou enlightens us through him.

And he is beautiful and radiant with a great splendor,
of Thee, Most High, does he convey the meaning.

- **Francesco Petrarca** is well-known for his contributions to poetry: the Petrarchan sonnet form and a whole lot of love poems. If you want to ponder the great Italian passion, amore, check out his Canzione. Here's a stanza from one of the said love poems:

  It was the day the sun's ray had turned pale
  With pity for the suffering of his Maker
  When I was caught, and I put up no fight,
  My lady, for your lovely eyes had bound me.

- Consider this quote from the Italian poet **Cesare Pavese** and discuss it together: *"Religion consists of the belief that everything that happens to us is extraordinarily important. It can never disappear from the world for this reason."*

If you and your friends are the crafty types, here are a couple of ideas for crafts to do while chatting:

- **Paint olive oil dispensers.** Buy oil dispensers at craft stores, along with paintbrushes and acrylic paints. The ambitious among you can paint Tuscan landscapes, grapevines, and sunflowers, while the more artistically challenged can paint red and white checkerboard patterns across the bottoms and tops of the bottles.

- **Stencil flour-sack dish towels or solid aprons** (found at craft stores). Buy stencils with grapevines, sunflowers, or other pictures with an Italian flair at a craft store, along with fabric paint and stencil brushes. Have masking tape on hand to tape the stencils to the towels or aprons. Your friends can give their creations as gifts or keep them as a remembrance of the great time you had together.

Book Club

Under the Tuscan Sun by Frances Mayes. The story of the author buying an estate in Tuscany and struggling to figure out life in a foreign country.

Paradiso by Dante Alighieri. A poetic masterpiece, Dante's journey through his vision of heaven.

Summer

Let's Go Fly a Kite: Freedom Picnic

- A service project for a small or large group
- A great way to meet new friends

This celebration at the park is your chance to have a great time with your friends *and* fight for freedom. This party is a little different—while enjoying a fun picnic, you and your friends will also work together to fight for women who can't celebrate the same freedoms you do. Read on to find out how. This party is great for a small group that wants to cement those friendships while playing and that also wants to engage in a meaningful service project to help women across the globe.

Menu :::::::::::::::::::

You don't want to fuss with a lot of spoons and plates at a picnic, so all your picnic fare can be eaten with just the hands and will fit nicely in your picnic basket. Bring along a cutting board and knife to slice up the sandwich.

Pressed Sandwich Italiano

This sandwich has a lot of zing and is an easy way to serve a crowd—You'll make one huge sandwich, press it with a heavy book, and slice it up at the picnic.

- ○ 1 flat loaf ciabatta bread or Italian rustic bread
- ○ ½ pound sliced salami
- ○ ½ pound pastrami
- ○ ¼ pound provolone
- ○ ¼ cup sweet onion slices
- ○ 16-ounce jar of roasted red peppers, drained and sliced
- ○ 8-ounce jar of marinated artichoke hearts, drained and sliced
- ○ ¼ cup olive oil
- ○ 1 tablespoon balsamic vinegar
- ○ 2 teaspoons oregano
- ○ salt and pepper

Slice the loaf of bread in half horizontally. If the bread is very thick, remove some of the bread from the center so the sandwiches aren't too thick. Layer the salami and pastrami on the bottom half of the loaf. In a bowl, mix olive oil, vinegar, and oregano. Spread oil mixture over bottom half of loaf and sprinkle with salt and freshly ground pepper.

Next layer the provolone on the sandwich, then the onion, red peppers, and artichoke hearts. Replace the top of the loaf. Then wrap the sandwich in parchment paper or cling wrap. Place the loaf on a cutting board, and place a heavy cast-iron skillet or brick or thick book on top. Place in refrigerator and chill and press for at least one hour. When ready to eat, remove plastic wrap and slice. Serves 8.

Sweet Corn Zucchini Boats

No spoons needed! These boats contain a sweet, fresh salad that make picnicking easy. And they're a good way to use up a bounty of July zucchini.

- ○ 2 zucchini, plus 1 cup chopped zucchini
- ○ 4 ears of sweet corn
- ○ 16 ounces grape tomatoes, halved
- ○ ½ cup chopped onion

- ○ 1 tablespoon olive oil
- ○ 1 teaspoon balsamic vinegar
- ○ 1 teaspoon sugar
- ○ ¼ cup fresh basil leaves, chopped
- ○ salt

Slice the corn off the ears; cook in boiling water for 3 minutes. Drain corn and cool. In a large bowl, combine 1 cup chopped zucchini, corn, tomatoes, onion, oil, vinegar, sugar, and basil.

Cut both zucchini in half lengthwise and horizontally, forming eight pieces. Remove pulp with a spoon, creating boats, leaving a thin layer of meat. Heap the corn mixture into each boat, and sprinkle with salt. Wrap each boat in plastic wrap to transport. Serves 8.

Cut both zucchini in half lengthwise and horizontally, forming eight pieces like this.

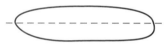 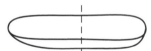

Watermelon Pops

You'll feel like schoolgirls again, savoring these fun summery pops.

- ○ one 2-pound seedless red watermelon
- ○ one 2-pound seedless yellow watermelon

- ○ 8 Popsicle sticks

Cut the rind off of the watermelon. Cut melon into 1-inch cubes. Insert sticks into slices, alternating colors. Freeze for at least one hour before serving. Serves 8.

Party Tip

Cut the watermelon using simple cookie-cutter shapes, such as circles or stars.

The Best Oatmeal Cookies

These cookies are from Celeste Gardiner, the gracious innkeeper at the Apple Orchard Inn in Durango, Colorado. They are, indeed, the best oatmeal cookies.

- 3 eggs, beaten
- 1 cup raisins
- 1 teaspoon vanilla
- 1 cup butter, softened
- 1 cup brown sugar
- 1 cup white sugar
- 3 cups all-purpose flour
- 1 teaspoon salt
- 1 teaspoon cinnamon
- 2 teaspoons baking soda
- 2 cups old-fashioned oatmeal
- 1 cup chopped pecans
- 1 cup butterscotch pieces

Soak raisins in eggs and vanilla for at least one hour. Cream butter and sugars together until fluffy. Add to the raisin mixture. Then add the dry ingredients and mix. Add the pecans and butterscotch pieces, mixing just until blended.

Bake at 375 degrees for 8 to 10 minutes. Makes about 4 dozen.

Pucker-Up Punch

Don't worry, this is an easy one. And it's a great use for those tart cherries falling in your back yard. If you don't have a cherry tree, visit a farmer's market for pie cherries.

- 12-ounce can frozen pink lemonade concentrate
- 1 cup frozen strawberries, thawed
- 3 cups tart cherries or pie cherries
- 1 quart ginger ale

Layer cherries on a baking sheet and freeze. Prepare lemonade according to package directions, and mix in ginger ale. Crush strawberries and stir into lemonade. Before serving, plop the frozen cherries into the lemonade for colorful "ice cubes."

Adding Pizzazz ....

The pizzazz this month isn't fancy centerpieces and mood music—it's you and your friends and the passion you can bring to fighting for a worthy cause. Consider these disturbing facts about freedom:

- **Twenty-seven million people worldwide are victims of forced labor.**

- *At least* **600,000 to 800,000 people are trafficked** each year and forced into slave labor—very often prostitution.

- **Of those trafficked, 80 percent are women and children.**

- **Women and children throughout the world are kidnapped or coerced** and forced into sex slavery. Some are forced to see up to 40 "clients" a day. Many are promised high-paying jobs in foreign countries. When they arrive at these "jobs," their identification and money are taken from them, and they are intimidated into silence. Some are beaten. Some are raped. Some are locked in. All are in desperate need of help.

Slavery *still* thrives in the world today, especially in some of the poorest countries. Children are trafficked and forced to become laborers and soldiers. Women and children are forced to be sex slaves in brothels. Visit these Web sites to find out more: **www.jfci.org** and **www.ijm.org**.

It's hard to know how to help when faced with an issue so large and so out of your control. But there *are* ways you can help. Talk to your friends about this huge issue before your picnic. If you're doing this with your small group, have a meeting in which you learn about the problem and commit to do something to help. You could do a Bible study focusing on Christians who have fought to stop slavery in the past. You could do a Bible study in which you explain the facts about slavery today to your friends and then study verses that discuss Christian responses. Then make commitments to do something to fight. Generate enthusiasm for your freedom picnic by talking often about how you and your friends are going to fight to make a difference.

Consider doing these options at your picnic:

Party Tip

Here are some verses to read and meditate on before, during, and after your picnic:
Psalm 9:17-19
Psalm 10:12
Psalm 72:12-13
1 John 3:17
James 4:17

- **Pray.** By all means, pray. Whatever else you decide to do, pray. Before engaging in your other plans for the picnic, pray and ask God to bless your efforts and get other people out there praying and helping.

- **Set aside a chunk of time to pray together as a group** after eating and before playing.

  Pray for the women and children who have been rescued from slavery and are now receiving aftercare, that God would heal their wounds. After spending time in a brutal situation, one's perspective on God, love, and the world is warped. Pray that aftercare workers would help victims make a healthy transition back into society.

  Pray for those currently caught in slavery. Pray that they would be rescued and that in the meantime, God would keep a flicker of hope alive in them.

  Pray for those in danger of being trafficked. Pray that they wouldn't be coerced into unsafe situations. Pray for awareness—that those in danger of being trafficked would learn about the false claims of traffickers (offering jobs in foreign countries) and that those with political power would be moved to take action against trafficking.

  And pray for the perpetrators. Pray that God would break through to their hearts just as he did with John Newton, the British slave-ship captain who, changed by God, went on to fight slavery and write the hymn "Amazing Grace."

- **Raise awareness during your picnic.** Many people have never heard of the problem of human trafficking. Put together informational fliers to pass out at the park with pertinent facts, things to pray for, and Web sites to visit for more information.

- **Help with a petition.** I haven't included information about a specific petition to get signed, as these will change. Visit the above Web sites to find out about petitions that need to be signed, which you and your friends can rally support for. Set up a booth, or approach people in the park with the petition and information about human trafficking. Contact your local city to find out rules about setting up a booth and getting petitions signed in a public location. If you have a booth, have Popsicles or cookies to draw people in.

- **Set up a lemonade stand.** Or, better yet, have a bake sale. The recipe for oatmeal cookies makes a large batch, so you'll have leftovers anyway! Have informational fliers at your stand, and ask for donations at your bake sale or lemonade stand. Again, contact your city to find out about where you're allowed to do this. If it's not legal in the park but your church is next to a park, set up your stand on church property.

- **Arrange to have a speaker come to your church** to tell people more about the problem. (Go to www.ijm.org to find a speaker.) Pass out fliers at the park with the date and time of the speaker's visit.

- **Get more great ideas** for how to help at the Web sites above.

- **After your picnic, go to a friend's house** to watch *Amazing Grace*, a 2007 Walden media movie about William Wilberforce, the English abolitionist who started a movement to end slavery. Afterward, discuss what you as a group can continue to do to fight for freedom.

Debriefing Questions

After your day in the park, it's a good idea to talk about what you all experienced. Here are some "debriefing" questions to discuss:

- How does learning about all of the huge issues out there, such as slavery, make you feel? Overwhelmed? Incensed? Discouraged? Motivated?

- How did it feel to just get out there and do something for what you think is right?

- Why do you think God allows things like slavery to occur in our world?

- How does reading the Psalms, such as Psalm 9:17-19 and Psalm 72:12-13, encourage you?

- Do you feel inspired to take action in the future about slavery or another issue that is on your heart? If so, what will you do?

Bring in the Entertainment! ::::::::::::::::::::

One of my favorite memories from childhood is watching the scene from *Mary Poppins* in which everyone abandons their work and worries to run to the park and fly a kite. *Let's go fly a kite, up to the highest height. Let's go fly a kite, and send it soaring.* Ah, I remember feeling so carefree watching that happy scene. And flying a kite always makes you feel carefree and childlike. You're going to be considering and praying about some heavy stuff during your day at the park. So, to lift the spirits, fly a kite! Have each woman bring her own kite, and sail away.

What if there's no wind, you ask? Surprise your friends with a water-balloon or water-gun fight. Or break out the glider airplanes, Frisbee, soccer ball, volleyball, or Rollerblades. Whatever will make you feel like kids again.

Book Club :::::::::::::::::::

The Natashas: Inside the New Global Sex Trade by Victor Malarek. If you'd like to find out more about the new slavery.

Hero for Humanity: A Biography of William Wilberforce by Kevin Belmonte. Biography of the English abolitionist.

Reading Lolita in Tehran: A Memoir in Books by Azar Nafisi. The story of eight women who met in secret in Tehran to read the classics, and found freedom in knowledge.

Southwest Cowgirl Campfire

As a Colorado girl, I couldn't write this book without including a campout. I think all of us at some time dream of the Old West and big skies and cowboy boots. No matter where you hang your hat, capture the joy of the smell of a campfire, the sound of camp songs, and the blanket of stars on an ink-black sky.

You can adapt this party however you'd like: I'll give you tips to create a cookout in your back yard; you can pull those tents out for an overnight backyard bash or you can head for the hills, mountains, lakes, seashore—whatever you've got. Some of the best conversations and moments happen around a campfire, singing songs and enjoying the late summer weather. This is a great party for getting back to your roots (or someone else's) and remembering the simple joys.

Menu

Party Tip

If it's still blazingly hot in your neck of the woods when you throw this party, call it a cookout rather than a campfire and it will sound much more appealing to your guests!

Instead of the old hot dog routine, give your cookout some kick with Southwest flair. The corn will be at its sweetest in August, and the spicy butter adds a tasty twist to a favorite. You've never had burgers like this before, and in my humble opinion, my guacamole is the best in the West.

Mint Limeade

The mint makes this simple party drink extra refreshing.

- 12-ounce container frozen limeade concentrate
- one bunch of mint (about 1 ounce)

Prepare limeade per package instructions in a large pitcher. Wash mint. About 30 minutes before serving, take small sprigs of mint and crush gently in hand, then stir into limeade. (For stronger mint flavor, put mint in earlier.) If you wish, place one sprig of mint in each person's glass. Makes 8 servings.

Baked Tortilla Chips

Fresh-baked tortilla chips are so tasty—and are healthier than store-bought!

- 20-ounce package flour tortillas
- no-fat cooking spray
- coarse sea salt
- lime juice
- cayenne or cumin

Preheat oven to 375 degrees. Spray baking sheet with cooking spray. Using kitchen shears, cut each tortilla into triangle wedges. Lay chips on baking sheet and spray with cooking spray. Sprinkle salt over chips, to taste. Squeeze a small bit of lime juice onto each chip. If desired, sprinkle chips with cumin or cayenne or a mix. Use the spices sparingly. Bake for 10 to 12 minutes, until golden. Can be made in advance and stored in an airtight container. Makes 8 servings.

Fastest Guac in the West

According to this cowgirl, one shouldn't mess with the pure goodness of an avocado by adding a lot of other vegetables to it.

- 4 avocados, peeled and pitted
- 2 teaspoons lime juice
- ½ teaspoon salt
- ½ teaspoon garlic powder
- ½ teaspoon dried cilantro
- ¼ teaspoon black pepper
- ¼ teaspoon Tabasco sauce
- ⅛ teaspoon cumin
- cayenne to taste

Mash avocados to desired consistency. Add the spices (except cayenne), and mix. Add pinches of cayenne until desired heat is reached. (I probably add at least ⅛ teaspoon.) Makes about 4 cups dip.

Grilled Corn on the Cob With Santa Fe Spice Butter

Sweet corn in August—could there be anything better? Yes, sweet corn with this spicy butter!

- 8 ears of corn, shucked and washed
- vegetable oil

Brush grill with oil. Grill corn on high until done, about 12 minutes, rotating often. Brush with Santa Fe Spice Butter. Serves 8.

Santa Fe Spice Butter

- 4 tablespoons butter
- 1 teaspoon lime juice
- ⅛ teaspoon salt
- ½ teaspoon cumin
- ¼ to ½ teaspoon red pepper flakes
- ¼ teaspoon ground black pepper

Mix ingredients and brush over hot grilled corn.

Party Tip

As soon as corn is picked, the sugars in it begin turning to starch. That's why the fresher the corn, the sweeter it tastes. Try buying your corn fresh from a farm-side stand or a farmer's market. If your corn isn't freshly picked, you can ensure it stays moist when grilling by leaving the last layer of the husk on so the juices aren't all lost.

Grilled Cinnamon Peaches

These peaches are an easy and delicious extra for your party.

- 8 ripe peaches
- cinnamon
- brown sugar
- honey

Slice peaches in half and pit them. Sprinkle with cinnamon and sugar. Brush grill with oil, and grill on medium-high heat without moving for about 3 minutes per side, until browned. Warm honey and drizzle over peaches, if desired.

Green Chili Buffalo Burger With Chili Mayonnaise

Driving along the Colorado countryside, one of my favorite sights is a herd of buffalo grazing under the big blue sky. If you've never had buffalo, you're in for a treat. It's one of the healthiest ground meats out there—lower in calories, fat, and sodium than beef, pork, and even chicken. And buffalo are typically raised using humane practices.

Burgers

- 2 pounds ground buffalo
- 2 eggs, beaten
- ¼ cup milk
- 2 slices worth of bread crumbs
- ¼ cup chopped onion
- one 4-ounce can chopped mild green chilies
- ½ teaspoon salt
- ½ teaspoon pepper
- ¼ teaspoon cumin

Chili Mayonnaise

- ½ cup low-fat mayonnaise
- 2 large cloves garlic, minced
- 3 teaspoons chili powder
- ½ teaspoon cumin
- 2 pinches cayenne
- 1 teaspoon soy sauce
- 1 teaspoon Worcestershire sauce

Accoutrements

- 8 slices jack cheese
- 8 hamburger buns, toasted
- 1 to 2 tomatoes, sliced
- 1 red onion, sliced
- lettuce

Combine all ingredients for burgers except buffalo in a large bowl and mix. Add ground meat and gently combine. Don't overmix. Shape into eight patties. Grill or broil for 12 to 14 minutes, turning once. Top with jack cheese.

Combine mayonnaise, and next six ingredients to make chili mayonnaise. Spread over toasted buns. Serve with tomato and onion slices and lettuce.

Party Tip

Barbecue sauce stands up great to buffalo. Serve it on the side instead of ketchup. If you can't find buffalo in your neck of the woods, use 85 percent lean ground beef. This burger is also great served open-faced, smothered with green chili sauce.

Cinnamon and Coffee Terrine With Mexican Chocolate Ganache

OK, so no real cowgirl has probably ever eaten this while out on the range. But she ought to—it's delicious! (And easy to make, to boot.)

Ganache

- ○ 8 ounces semisweet chocolate chips
- ○ 1 teaspoon cinnamon
- ○ ⅛ teaspoon cayenne pepper
- ○ ½ teaspoon vanilla extract
- ○ ¾ cup heavy cream

Terrine

- ○ 2 cinnamon graham crackers
- ○ 1 pint light coffee ice cream
- ○ 1 quart (2 pints) light cinnamon ice cream

To make the ganache, combine the first four ingredients in a stainless steel bowl. In a saucepan over medium heat, bring the cream to a boil while stirring. Remove from heat and pour over the chocolate. Mix with a wooden spoon until melted and well blended. Let cool at room temperature until spreadable and cool (at least one hour). (Place in the fridge if you need to cool ganache faster.)

To make the terrine, put two layers of cling wrap lengthwise in a 9x5-inch loaf pan with several inches of overhang. Then put two layers of cling wrap widthwise, allowing five inches on each side for overlap. Let coffee ice cream sit out for 5 minutes, until softened. Spread softened coffee ice cream into the pan, and put back in freezer for 15 minutes.

When the ganache is well cooled, spread it on top of the coffee layer, and place back in freezer for 15 minutes (until ganache is hardened). Soften cinnamon ice cream, and spread it on top of ganache layer. Crumble the graham crackers on top, and press lightly into ice cream. Cover with overhanging cling wrap. Freeze for several hours before serving; can be made three days in advance. When serving, use cling wrap to lift terrine out of pan. Slice horizontally into 8 servings.

S'mores

If the great outdoors for your party isn't in your back yard but somewhere in them thar hills, you're not going to have a freezer for the ice-cream pie, of course. Well, the obvious solution is sometimes the best. Get out the graham crackers, marshmallows, and chocolate bars. You know what to do.

Party Tip

Don't be scared away by big fancy words like "terrine." This is basically a layered ice cream pie.

Party Tip

Here are some variations: If you can't find cinnamon ice cream, stir 1 teaspoon cinnamon into a softened quart of vanilla ice cream. If you're not a coffee fan, use dulce de leche ice cream instead. If you want a light dessert, layer half the amount of ganache.
This treat will look even more fabulous if you make the layers as follows: one layer cinnamon, one layer ganache, one layer coffee, one layer ganache, one layer cinnamon. (It'll just take a little longer to make.)

Summer

Campfire Bananas

If you want a change from S'mores, make Campfire Bananas. Leave the peel on, and slit bananas lengthwise on the inside of their curve. Insert chocolate chips, peanut butter chips, and marshmallows into the slit and cover in foil. Melt over the campfire and enjoy.

Adding Pizzazz

- **Let's start with the easy part.** Have your guests come dressed in their best Southwestern duds: boots, bolo ties, ropers, belt buckles, cowboy hats, turquoise jewelry, and so on.

- **It'll be easy to drift from a Southwestern to a Western feel at your party**—that's OK. Go for what you like and what you have available.

- **The next thing to decide is where you're going to have your cookout.** Your menu is transportable (just grill the corn and burgers on site), so you can host it anywhere. (In this case, have S'mores or Campfire Bananas, not the ice-cream terrine, for dessert.) Have your party at a campsite, at a national park, or at a park. If you'd like to make this a fun event to invite new friends to, make your location a fun destination, such as a campsite. In this case, you can keep decorating to a minimum. (Just make sure to check for any fire bans in effect.)

- **You can also create your cookout right in your own back yard.** Start with your campfire. Here's how to make a fire pit: Determine where you'd like your fire pit to be—away from anything flammable and on dirt. Dig down about nine inches. Then make a foot-high border around it using large rocks or bricks. Layer your logs in the pit.

- **Even if you can't have a real fire in your locale,** make a fire pit by creating a rock or brick border about a foot high and then laying logs inside your pit. It'll be a charming conversation starter and a place for your guests to gather around. You could even add twinkle lights or battery-operated tea lights for a bit of cheer.

- **Your fire pit or campfire will probably be the focal point of the party** (it's like the TV or kitchen—people gravitate toward it). So, set up seating around the fire pit. If you can, obtain bales of hay from local farms for guests to sit on. Layer horse blankets over the hay as padding. Or if you have camp chairs, use these instead of your patio furniture. You can also use large logs or rocks for seating.

- **Put red and white checked tablecloths on your tables** and use old camping lanterns for your lighting. If you don't have any lanterns, place white votive candles or pillar candles in mason jars and light.

Party Tip

If you have a Texas-sized budget, just invest in a store-bought fire pit!

- **For your next layer of decorating, set up tents.** You can have them tucked out of the way to add ambience. Or, better yet, make your party a true campout in the back yard. If you want to make this a family event, spend the night sleeping under the stars or in tents. It'll be great fun for the kids and an event they're sure to remember.

- **Make your decorations whimsical and easy.** Wind a rope to look like a lasso, and hang it on the back of a chair. If you have access to a saddle, set it out.

- **If you want your guests to feel that they truly stumbled upon a Southwestern camp,** pin up a drying line between a couple of trees. Attach socks, undershirts, and long underwear to the line with clothespins.

- **Set cowboy hats (found at party stores) about the place.** You can also find many other Western-themed decorations at party stores. Keep your eyes open for wagon wheels, cactus cutouts, and toy guns.

- **If you'd like to have a favor for each guest,** bundle up treats in red and white bandannas. You could even attach the bandannas to a stick (hobo-style) for the guests to carry. Include things such as beef jerky, hot sauces, dried fruits, sheriff badges, and toy harmonicas. I can just hear you and all your guests harmonizing over the campfire with your harmonicas.

- **To make your guests feel extra loved,** make favors such as prickly pear jelly or homemade salsa.

- **Food is always my favorite decoration.** Place piles of peaches in wooden buckets and cluster ears of unshucked corn by the baskets.

- And, of course, have **country western music** playing in the background.

Bring in the Entertainment!

Your entertainment can be as simple as singing some camp songs or praise songs to the tune of a harmonica, or you can use the ideas below.

Corn-Shucking Competition

If you're having a larger party or if you just eat a whole lot of corn, have your guests do the hard work for you by having a corn-shucking competition. Set up a table with the piles of corn and a bucket of water for each contestant to place the shucked corn in. You can make it a timed competition and see who shucks the most in a certain amount of time, or see who completes shucking a certain amount of corn first. Rally excitement by having fun trophies or prizes for the ultimate corn shucker. You can have a T-shirt made that says "Corn Shucking Queen" as a prize, or a bottle of popcorn with popcorn seasonings or a popcorn maker as a prize. Or be as resourceful as those Old Western folk, and create a corncob trophy.

Party Tip

If you'd like to *really* get closer with those girlfriends, a night in a tent under the stars is a truly bonding experience.

Queen of Fire

By now most of your guests have watched *Survivor* or some similar show and scoffed at how inept the participants were at making fire. Find out who among your guests is the Queen of Fire by having a fire-starting competition. If you want to make it educational, give a short demonstration first on how to start fire. Set up three or more stations for your competitors with what they'll need: a magnesium and flint block, and dry kindling such as pine needles, dryer lint, or dry twigs. The idea is to get sparks of flame created by scraping the flint against the block to land on the kindling to start the fire. Whoever is the first to get a flame wins. If you're having a real fire, you could do this competition before starting it and use the winner's flame to light your fire.

Party Tip

An appropriate crown for your Queen of Fire would be a Native American chief's headdress from a toy store.

Storytelling

Campfires draw out people's stories. Staring at the glowing embers, the stories stream out of us like the snaking trails of smoke above a fire. If you have a larger group, you may want to form smaller groups to share stories. If you're in a smaller group, share your stories all together. Consider having each person answer some of these questions:

- What's your favorite memory of being in the great outdoors?

- Tell your best or worst camping story.

- If you lived in the Old West, which would you most like to be: a cowgirl riding free on the range? a Native American living simply off the land? part of the cavalry? a pioneer starting a whole new life? Why?

- What main feeling strikes you when you're out in nature—do you feel small? Do you feel wonder at the Creator? Do you feel scared? Are you completely content? Do you wish you'd brought the mosquito repellent along? Tell a story about a time you felt one of these ways.

- Tell about a time being in nature made you realize how big the universe around you is or the possibilities it holds (such as God or angels or mystery).

- What's one thing you're more likely to believe in when you're surrounded by God's creation?

- When you stare up at an inky black sky blanketed with infinite stars, what do you feel? What does it reveal to you about the nature of the universe?

- Living in cities with flooding light all the time, what effect do you think it has had on our worldviews that we no longer nightly see the stars and the sky in their vast expanse?

- Why do you think God created all of the stars in their infinity and not just the Earth? What can you learn from this?

I Was There

To get in the storytelling mood, you can also play the "I Was There" game. Start everyone out with a fun story, such as, "I was walking in the woods the other day when all of a sudden an eagle swooped down and plucked the apple I was eating from my hand." Then someone interjects, "I was there!" and continues the story. For example, "I was there, and saw you start wrestling with the eagle. Because it wasn't an apple in your hand, it was chocolate, and boy, were you mad." (Someone else) "I was there! And I saw a squirrel scamper out from the trees and steal the chocolate while you and the eagle were busy batting each other. Then the squirrel ate it and turned into a beautiful princess." OK, so hopefully your story will be better than mine, but you get the picture, right?

Cowgirl Memories

If you have time, one of the best things to do is to have people simply tell their life stories. Most everyone loves talking about herself. Tell where you came from, what you've done, where you're going, what your dreams are. This is an incredible way to get personal with one another. This would also be a great time to share your faith stories. Tell when and how you first found Jesus and what roads you've journeyed together thus far. Just make sure everyone gets a turn. (You may want to get into smaller groups for this.)

Book Club

Redeeming Love by Francine Rivers. The story of the book of Hosea, of God's love and pursuit of us, told in the setting of the Old West.

My Ántonia by Willa Cather. One of the all-time great American pioneer novels. And, OK, so it takes place in Nebraska, not exactly the southwest. But if you're in New York, it's southwest from *you*, right?

Fall

The Great Adventure Party

- Great for large-group or small-group bonding
- Can be done at any time of the year
- Fun outreach night

The story of the universe is a story of adventure: A perfect kingdom and King, a revolt and war, long years of refugees journeying through unknown lands and facing perils, a prince from afar risking all to rescue his love, and, lastly, a joyous wedding with the long-lost love. Sounds like any dime-store adventure or romance book, doesn't it?

This story of adventure, the true story of the universe, is imprinted on each of our hearts. Each of our hearts longs for adventure and greatness and for a Rescuer because we know this is the story of our lives. Awaken in your friends the thirst for adventure and what that thirst ultimately points to. Set aside a day or night for adventure—don't underestimate the serious bonding effect it can have on your friendships. If you decide to go out for an adventure, such as rafting, this is a great experience for your whole women's ministry! (Just get help with the food!)

Party Tip

Does your region have an eccentric dish that you and your friends have never dared trying yet? Now's the time! If you live in the mountains, fry up some Rocky Mountain Oysters (hint: they're not oysters). If you're in the wetlands, how about some frog-leg soup? Or, to be a bit more sophisticated, try a dish such as caviar, escargot, or steak tartare.

Menu

This menu is made up of delicious, adventurous recipes. The recipes have surprising ingredients that your friends won't expect. The dishes are Moroccan-, Indonesian-, and Indian-inspired and will be a tasty new venture for your friends. Before eating, tell them the foreign names of the dishes, such as the Es Alpukat and the B'stilla, but not what they are. It'll take bravery to taste, but they'll be richly rewarded with a delicious meal.

Es Alpukat
(Mocha Avocado Chiller)

There's avocado in this shakelike drink. The recipe is based on an Indonesian drink that gets its rich consistency from the avocado. Serve when guests arrive. (The Indonesian drink wouldn't have chocolate milk in it, but I won't tell if you don't.)

- ○ 2 ripe avocados, pitted and peeled
- ○ 4 cups strong brewed coffee, chilled
- ○ 2 cups chocolate milk
- ○ 8 cups ice cubes

Combine ingredients in blender and blend until smooth, about 1 minute. You may need to make in several batches.

North African Tomato Soup

Serve this soup chilled as a first course. The North African spices and honey make this not your average tomato soup. If you want to save time on party day, make this a day ahead and store it in the fridge—the flavors will have a chance to combine this way.

- ○ 2 pound tomatoes, chopped (food processor works well)
- ○ 1 large onion, chopped
- ○ 3 tablespoons olive oil
- ○ 2 teaspoon paprika
- ○ ½ teaspoon ginger
- ○ ½ teaspoon cumin
- ○ ½ teaspoon cinnamon
- ○ ½ teaspoon dried cilantro
- ○ 2 cups chicken broth
- ○ 4 teaspoons honey
- ○ salt and pepper

In a medium saucepan, heat olive oil over medium heat. Add onion and sauté for 3 to 4 minutes, or until softened. Add spices (next 5 ingredients) and cook for 1 additional minute. Add tomatoes, broth, and honey and bring to a boil. Remove from heat and let cool. Puree in a food processor, and salt and pepper to taste. Refrigerate until serving. Serves 8.

B'stilla (Moroccan Chicken Pastry)

Mmm, I still remember the first time I had B'stilla. You break the pastry with your fingers, and steam escapes carrying the luxurious scents of almonds, cinnamon, and chicken to your nostrils. This will be an experience you and your friends won't forget. This dish takes a little longer to prepare, so the other recipes are fairly simple. Spend your extra time making this dish that is an event unto itself!

- ○ 3 tablespoons butter
- ○ ½ cup onion, chopped
- ○ 1 clove garlic, minced
- ○ ¼ teaspoon black pepper
- ○ ½ teaspoon salt
- ○ ¼ teaspoon ground ginger
- ○ 1 teaspoon cinnamon
- ○ ¼ teaspoon cumin
- ○ 1 pound skinless, boneless chicken breasts
- ○ ¾ cup chicken broth
- ○ 4 ounces almonds (about ¾ cup)
- ○ ½ cup powdered sugar
- ○ 2 eggs, beaten
- ○ 2 sheets (1 package) frozen puff pastry, fully thawed

Topping

- ○ 2 tablespoons butter
- ○ 2 tablespoons powdered sugar
- ○ ½ teaspoon cinnamon

Melt 3 tablespoons butter in a large saucepan over medium heat. Add onions and garlic, and sauté for 4 minutes. Add next 5 ingredients and sauté for 1 minute. Add chicken and broth, and simmer covered for 25 minutes, until chicken is cooked through.

Remove chicken from the pan, keeping broth warm on stove. Shred chicken using two forks and return to the pan. Bring broth to a boil and heat until liquid is greatly reduced. In the meantime, finely chop the almonds and mix with the ½ cup of powdered sugar. In a large bowl, mix half of the almond mixture, all the chicken mixture, and the beaten eggs.

Party Tip

This B'stilla will feed six. Serve it on one large platter that women will all eat from, using their fingers. If your friends aren't so into eating with their fingers from the same plate, you can bail them out after a minute of trying it.

Step-by-Step

1.

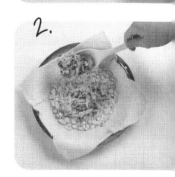

2.

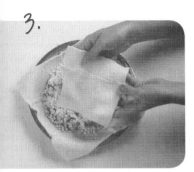
3.

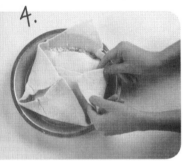
4.

5.

Spread one sheet of puff pastry in a 9-inch pie plate. Divide the remaining pastry sheet into quarters, and reserve three quarters for another use (Step 1). Roll the remaining quarter out to a 6-inch square. Layer half of the remaining almond mixture on the bottom of the dish, leaving an inch around the edge of the pastry. Next layer the chicken mixture. Then layer the rest of the almond mixture (Step 2). Cover this layer with the remaining pastry sheet (Step 3). Fold the edges of the bottom sheet over the top (Step 4) and pinch the openings shut (Step 5).

Melt the remaining 2 tablespoons of butter, and brush the top of the pastry. Bake for 35-40 minutes at 350 degrees, until pastry is golden brown. Let cool for 15 to 20 minutes before serving. Sprinkle with remaining powdered sugar and cinnamon. Serves 6.

Moroccan-Spiced Carrots

These carrots are a quick and easy side to your main dish and are a subtle twist on a North American favorite, glazed carrots.

- O 2 pounds carrots
- O 1½ tablespoons butter
- O 2 tablespoons brown sugar
- O ½ cup water
- O 2 teaspoons lemon juice
- O ½ teaspoon salt
- O ¼ teaspoon cinnamon
- O ⅛ teaspoon cayenne

Cut carrots into 2-inch slices. Heat butter in a medium pan. Add carrots and sauté for 5 minutes, until tender. Add the brown sugar and stir until melted. Add the remaining ingredients and simmer, covered, for another 8 minutes, until carrots are well glazed. Serve warm. Serves 8.

Aam ki Kulfi
(Indian Mango Ice Cream)

This is a much simplified recipe of the ice cream that would be served to Moghul emperors in the 1500s.

- O 12 ounces evaporated milk
- O ½ cup dried milk powder
- O ¾ cup sugar
- O 3 cups fresh cubed mango (about 3 large mangoes)
- O ½ teaspoon ground
- cardamom
- O ¼ cup chopped pistachios (optional)

In a food processor, puree mangoes. Add evaporated milk, milk powder, sugar, and cardamom and blend. Pour into eight ramekins (or kulfi molds if you happen to have them!). If you don't have ramekins, use ice-cube trays, and give each guest

Party Tip

If you can't find ripe mangoes, sliced frozen mangoes taste great, too.

several. The shape of this dessert will make it adventurous, so freeze it in whatever odd-shaped dishes you have—conical, square, or a parfait dish (kulfi dishes are often pyramid-shaped).

Freeze 4-5 hours or overnight. (I prefer it only frozen about 4 hours so it's not as icy.) Set in the fridge 20 minutes before serving. Dip in cool water. Unmold onto serving plates and top with pistachios.

Adding Pizzazz

To make your dining experience an adventure for your friends, change small things in your dining setup. Here are a few ideas:

- **Instead of paper napkins,** when your guests sit down, give them each a clean towel to drape over their shoulders. The B'stilla can be messy, so they'll be grateful for the towel close at hand to dab their mouths and hands. (Towels draped over one shoulder is the traditional Moroccan "napkin.")
- **Turn off all the lights,** and solely light your room with candles. Buy bunches of small votives, and set them around the edges of your dining area and on the center of the table.
- **Dine while lounging on the floor.** Eat at a low table or a coffee table. If you have a large, patterned area rug, place it on the floor under your table. Place lots of plump colorful pillows on the floor so your friends can make themselves comfy while eating.
- **Drape colorful sheets from the ceiling,** giving your room a cozy Moroccan feel.
- **Have incense burning** when women arrive to give your place a mysterious ambience.
- **Have music from another country playing in the background**—Indian, Middle Eastern, African, Asian, whatever you can find! Putumayo World Music is a company that specializes in CDs of music from all cultures, and their music is great fun! Check out their selection at www.putumayo.com.

Party Tip

If you'd like to serve a drink on the side, try mint tea (a common Moroccan beverage). It will complement the main dish well and has such an exotic aroma! For an easy side dish, buy up all those exotic fruits from the grocery store. You know, the ones you point to and say, "What's *that*?!!"

Bring in the Entertainment!

There are endless possibilities of adventures for you and your friends to brave together. First, think about what level of adventurers you all are: Novices, Journeywomen, or Extremers. If you're Novices, you prefer the tamer waters; if you're Journeywomen, you're ready for a thrill; if you're Extremers, you live for a serious adrenaline rush. You can have adventures at your home, or you can plan a fun day out after or before your meal. Here are some ideas for days out:

Novices

- Take a float trip down a nearby river (a tame version of river rafting).
- Go for a train ride. (Many mountain or tourist areas have day train trips.)
- Take a hot-air balloon ride together.
- If you choose to do this in the winter, go on a sleigh ride, go sledding, or go ice skating on a lake.

Journeywomen

- Go jeeping—on your own or a guided tour.
- Go canoeing.
- Rent a speedboat and go water skiing.
- Go rappelling.

Extremers

- Go white-water river rafting.
- Go skydiving.
- Go kayaking.
- Go rock climbing.
- Go ice climbing (in the winter).

And then there's the adventure of learning something new. Here are some things you and your friends can learn to do together:

- **Take a dance class together:** belly dancing, ballroom, salsa, hip-hop— whatever is your speed.
- **Go on a guided fly-fishing tour together.**
- **Take a language class together.** (Next time you get sushi, you can order in Japanese!)
- **Take a cooking class together,** perhaps an ethnic cuisine course.
- **If technology is a four-letter word to you and your friends,** take a computer class together or learn the newest technology together.

There also may be companies in your area that specialize in adventure. Look for companies that provide team-building experiences, such as ropes courses. If you'd rather stay in than go out, there are even adventurous experiences to have indoors. Here are some fun ideas for staying in:

- **Create henna body art (often called henna tattooing).** Henna tattooing is practiced throughout the world, but is best known by Americans as an Indian art. Indian brides tattoo themselves before their weddings. Henna is a plant dye that is painted on in intricate designs. It washes off within one to four weeks. Your "tattoos" will seem quite adventurous for those couple of weeks! You can find many books on henna tattooing at most bookstores and can order henna supplies online.
- **If henna tattoos are a little *too* adventurous for you, take a smaller step out of your box with adventurous makeovers.** You could go totally wild and crazy and go for platinum blonde (just like I've been secretly dreaming of for years now).

Or buy temporary color washes for each other's hair. Spend the night helping one another with the dyes or washes. You could follow up your adventurous hair with some bright red toenails and some silver eye shadow, too!

- **Have an adventurous spa night together.** Picture this: an avocado carrot mask, a chocolate face mask, a coffee body scrub, a rosemary honey hair conditioner. Search online for at-home spa recipes.

- **Have an adventurous night of worshipping God together.** If you've been doing the same pattern of worship for years in your ministry, try something new! Worship should be an experience. Set up meditative prayer stations around your area, using objects at each area to prompt responses in your friends. For example, at one station you might have several small pumpkins. Have the women hold the pumpkins and consider what it prompts in them and how that relates to their relationship to God. It might remind one woman of her grandmother's pie and how much holidays and her family mean to her. She would then spend time praying, thanking God for her family and praying for them. It might remind another woman of the fall and the ending of the year. She might meditate on the seasons of life, how things grow, then die. She could then thank God for the life he's given her and pray to be thankful for each day.

Other objects you might set out are a mirror, a flower, a blanket, a teddy bear. Use objects that are very touchable and that evoke emotions. After women go through your prayer stations, you can gather together and share about your experiences, if your guests are comfortable doing so. Or, instead of individual prayer stations, have a group prayer session that's a little out of the box. Pray together in a submissive posture, such as with your faces on the ground or on your knees holding hands. It might be out of women's comfort zones, but it can bring new depth, intimacy, and authenticity to praying together.

You can also have adventurous worship through music or dance or art. Perhaps one woman worships through poetry; she can read a poem for the group. Perhaps another worships through dance; have her lead the others in dance. For more resources for experiential worship, go to www.group.com.

Movie Time

If you find you need some inspiration before you and your girlfriends get out there in the saddle of adventure yourselves, you may want to watch one of these adventure movies together just for fun:

Lawrence of Arabia (1962)
The Treasure of the Sierra Madre (1948)
National Treasure (2004)
Raiders of the Lost Ark (1981)

Party Tip

Here are a few festivals going on around the country in the fall that can make you and your friends into brave, adventurous women:

- If you're in North Carolina, you're in luck. September holds the **Annual Bugfest** at the North Carolina Museum of Natural Sciences. Visit the Café Insecta to feast on silkworm hummus and scorpion stir fry. Visit www.bugfest.org.

- **Ever had fried frog legs?** Well, if you're in Louisiana, hop on over to the Rayne Frog Festival where you can try them out. www.rayne.org.

- **Or how about some roadkill?** Marlinton, West Virginia, will be holding its roadkill cookoff in September. Squirrel brains, here you come. www.pccoc .com/roadkill.cfm.

Gab Time

So what's the point of all this adventure stuff, you ask? Your adventures together will deepen your friendships with one another, but there's more to it than just that. Adventure is a fundamental part of each of our stories and is written onto each of our souls, even if we don't know it. The Bible is the recounting of the greatest story, the story of God's love for and pursuit of his people. We are each a part of that story.

God created us and wants to lavish us with his love. But we've been separated from him by our own sins. And the rest of the story is in his pursuit to regain us and our journey toward him. Our separation from God is ultimately the heart origin of all the deep longings within us. The desire for romance, for adventure, for love, for significance, for purpose, all these desires point to our need to reclaim our position as God's daughters, and to become Christ's bride. These longings will never be fulfilled on this earth, not as long as we're still separated from God. And that's OK. They are the reminders and the road signs that direct us and push us on in our journey toward God.

Talk with your friends about the hidden desires God has placed in each of your hearts. Here are some questions to discuss together:

- We yearn for adventure because there is a deep longing inside of us. When you desire adventure, what is it your soul is really thirsting for? Significance? Excitement? Purpose? Fun?

- What does this longing tell you about the way you were created?

- What has moved you lately—a movie, a book, a Hallmark commercial? What was the heart of that message that moved you, and what does it tell you about the deep desires in your heart?

- How do you usually respond to moments of deep longing or yearning? Do you think this is a good response? What would be the best response?

- Does your spiritual life currently feed or fulfill your deep yearnings?

- How can you use your desire for adventure as a fuel powering your journey toward God?

Book Club

The Sacred Romance by Brent Curtis and John Eldredge. This excellent Christian book explores the adventurous journey of the heart toward God.

The Adventures of Huckleberry Finn by Mark Twain. The amusing adventures of a young boy journeying down the Mississippi. Great fun.

Endurance by Alfred Lansing. The tale of Ernest Shackleton's voyage to Antarctica.

King Solomon's Mines by H. Rider Haggard. One of the great adventure classics—the adventure to find the lost treasures of King Solomon.

Murder at Kensington Manor

It's a dark and stormy night. You, Lady Poppington, have invited everyone who's anyone over to your posh estate in the English countryside, Kensington Manor, for a fall feast. The night is going swimmingly, when suddenly a scream pierces the cold night air. A murderer has struck. And all your guests are suspects…

Your murder mystery night will be different from other murder mystery events you might have gone to. The mystery is an easy game that will fit right in with your party—you don't need to worry about reading a script or having an exact number of guests. And, of course, you'll treat your guests to a rich fall feast. Everyone will have such a ball, you might even make it an annual event!

- Great for groups of 8 to 20
- Great outreach party

Menu

Enjoy a fall feast fit for a British manor. Your party will have the tempting smells of simmering cider and a savory butternut soup. Since you're serving dinner at the aristocratic Kensington Manor, serve your meal in courses. And if you've still left an inch of room after the trifle, guests can try their hands at their very own caramel apple creations.

Spiced Cider

The smell of apple cider warming will remind you and your friends of crisp fall nights.

- ○ 6 inches cinnamon stick, broken
- ○ ¼ teaspoon ground ginger
- ○ ¼ teaspoon allspice
- ○ peel from ½ orange
- ○ 1 teaspoon whole cloves
- ○ 8 cups of apple juice or cider
- ○ ¼ cup honey

Stick the orange peel with the cloves. In a large pot or crockpot, combine all ingredients. Bring to a boil; then simmer for 20 minutes.

Creamy Butternut Bisque

This rich soup is a perfect start to a meal on a cold fall night.

- ○ 1 tablespoon butter
- ○ 1 medium onion, chopped
- ○ 2 cloves garlic, minced
- ○ 1 butternut squash (about 2½ pounds)
- ○ 2 carrots, chopped
- ○ 4 cups chicken broth
- ○ ½ teaspoon salt
- ○ ½ teaspoon sage
- ○ 2 bay leafs
- ○ 1 cup heavy cream
- ○ freshly ground black pepper

Party Tip

Make the cider on the stove an hour before guests arrive. It permeates your party area with such a wonderful fall scent and is one less thing to worry about right before guests arrive. Just keep it on low heat on the stove. Make the bisque one day ahead to save time on party day and allow the flavors of the soup to meld. The trifle can also be made one day ahead.

Fall

Party Tip

If you have fresh sage, garnish bowls of the bisque with a few leaves. You can also swirl a small amount of cream on the top of each serving.

Party Tip

Eat your vegetables! Serve steamed vegetables, such as cauliflower, as an easy side to your tenderloin and potatoes. If you'd like to add a course to your meal, serve greens tossed with Gorgonzola and walnuts. Drizzle with a vinaigrette.

Halve squash, seed it, peel it, and cut into ½-inch pieces. Melt butter in large stockpot. Add onion and garlic and sauté for 3 minutes. Add squash and next 5 ingredients, and bring to a boil over high heat. Reduce heat to medium low and simmer, partially covered, about 25 minutes, until squash is fully cooked.

Puree soup in batches in a blender, and return to pan. Add cream and heat through. Salt and pepper to taste. Makes 10 servings.

Rosemary Pork Tenderloin With Apple Cream Sauce

This apple cream sauce is a nice twist to the classic pork and apple combination.

- ○ 2½ pounds pork tenderloin
- ○ 4 tablespoons fresh rosemary
- ○ 4 cloves of garlic, minced
- ○ 1 teaspoon salt
- ○ ½ teaspoon black pepper

Sauce
- ○ ²/₃ cup apple cider
- ○ 3 cups thinly sliced Braeburn apples (about 3 apples)
- ○ 1 cup whipping cream
- ○ lemon juice

Preheat oven to 400 degrees. Combine rosemary and garlic. Make several slits in pork, and place half of rosemary mixture in slits. Combine remaining rosemary mixture with salt and pepper. Rub pork with mixture. Place on a baking pan coated with cooking spray. Insert a meat thermometer into thickest portion of pork. Bake for 30 minutes or until a thermometer reaches 160 degrees. Let stand for 5 minutes; then cut into ¼-inch slices. Serve with sauce. Serves 8.

To make sauce, slice apples thinly and toss with lemon juice to stop browning. Heat cider in a pan over medium and cook 5 minutes, until reduced to ¹/₃ cup. Add apple slices and whipping cream, bring to a simmer, and cook over medium heat for 10 minutes, until sauce thickens and apple is tender. If sauce doesn't thicken, add a small amount of cornstarch and mix. Season with salt if desired. Serve over tenderloins.

Rosemary Roasted Potatoes

You can bake your potatoes on the same pan as your pork.

- ○ 6 large yukon gold potatoes (or 8 medium)
- ○ 2 tablespoons fresh rosemary

- ○ olive oil
- ○ freshly ground pepper
- ○ salt

Cut potatoes in 1-inch pieces, and place on large baking pan. Sprinkle with rosemary, salt, and pepper. Drizzle generously with olive oil. Toss well. Bake at 400 degrees for 30 minutes or until browned.

Gingerbread Pumpkin Trifle With Maple Whipped Cream and Candied Pecans

Finish your meal with an easy trifle that is the essence of fall comfort food.

- 1 package gingerbread mix (or 1 loaf store-bought gingerbread)
- one 4-ounce package vanilla pudding
- 2 cups milk
- 7 ounces pumpkin puree
- 2 tablespoons brown sugar
- ½ teaspoon pumpkin pie spice
- 1 cup whipping cream
- ¼ cup pure maple syrup (100%, not Aunt Jemima!)

Pecans
- ½ cup pecans, chopped
- 2 tablespoons brown sugar
- 1 tablespoon butter, melted

Prepare gingerbread according to package directions, let cool, then cut into 1-inch chunks. To make candied pecans, combine butter and brown sugar in a small saucepan and heat over medium. Stir in pecans and cook for 5 minutes. Spread on wax paper. Let cool and harden.

Prepare pudding according to package directions, and let cool. Add the pumpkin, sugar, and spice, and mix. In a chilled bowl, beat cold whipping cream with chilled beaters until peaks form. Add maple syrup and mix.

Cover the bottom of a large bowl with half of the gingerbread pieces. Top this with half of the pumpkin mixture, followed by half of the whipped cream. Repeat layers, and top with candied pecans. Trifle makes 12 servings.

Party Tip

You can also make the trifle in individual parfait cups.

Adding Pizzazz

Transform your party into an old English manor with just a few little touches.

- **If you have a long dining table with high-backed chairs, it would be just the thing.**
- **Serve on china and use silver candelabra for lighting.** Use whatever silver you have to serve.
- **Set out old British-looking knickknacks,** such as old dusty Shakespeare volumes, globes, tapestries, and big Turkish carpets.
- **Play classical music in the background.**
- **What you lack in estate décor, you can make up for with fall décor**—lots of pumpkins, winter squashes, and reds, yellows, and oranges.
- **To give some fancy oomph to fall décor,** add sparkle to your pumpkins. Buy several mini pumpkins, including white if you can find them. Buy several different colors of powder glitter, such as wine red, rust, and gold. Use a paintbrush to spread Elmer's

glue over an entire pumpkin. Over newspapers, sprinkle the pumpkins with glitter, coating evenly. Let dry, and then shake off excess glitter. These would make a classy centerpiece!

- **Ask your guests to come dressed as fine British aristocrats, the snootier the better.**
- **If you'd like to play up the murder mystery aspect of your party,** have the murder implements used in the game Clue as part of your table decoration: a candlestick, a rope, a revolver, a knife, a lead pipe, and a wrench.

Bring in the Entertainment!

Make-Your-Own Caramel Apples

I regularly press my nose against the windows of candy stores and drool at the over-the-top caramel apples. Make some big, bad apples of your own at your party. Let guests create their own caramel apples to take home or eat right there.

Have one or two apples per person. Buy bags of caramels from the grocery store (easy to find in the fall), and melt caramel according to package directions. Have various toppings for guests to dip their apples in, or ask each guest to bring her favorite topping. Here are some ideas: marshmallows, crushed graham crackers, melted chocolate, crushed Oreos, cinnamon candies, and M&Ms candies. Have cellophane bags ready for guests to put their finished apples in and ribbon to tie them closed. Or, if you eat them right away, have plenty of napkins ready. There's nothing more bonding than trying to eat fresh caramel apples in front of your friends. (It can be a bit messy!)

The Murder Mystery

The scene: a dinner party at Kensington Manor, a hoity-toity estate just outside of London. **The crime:** One by one, your guests are being murdered by the infamous Jenkings Jewelry Ring. **The suspects:** all your guests.

Your mystery will be based on a simple game that's easy to catch on to and hilarious to play. (You might recognize it—it's an adapted version of the game Mafia.) Each of your guests will choose a card from a deck, which they keep secret. To prepare:

- Put only one ace in the deck. Whoever draws the ace is the Investigator.
- Put only one 10 in the deck. Whoever gets the 10 is the Doctor.
- Whoever gets a face card is one of the murderers. If you have a group of around 8, you'll want 2 to be murderers, so put 2 face cards in the deck. If you have a group of around 20, you'll want 4 murderers, so put 4 face cards in the deck.
- Have the same number of cards as guests.

Explain the game to your guests: Whoever received a face card is part of **the infamous Jenkings Jewelry Ring**. This ring has come to the party tonight to abscond with the dazzling jewels your guests wore, and, one by one, they will try to murder the guests.

Whoever received the ace is **the Investigator**. This person can investigate one person at a time, asking you whether or not the person is one of the murderers.

Whoever received the 10 is **the Doctor**. This person can choose one person (including herself) to save in case the murderers choose to kill her.

To start the game, have your guests introduce themselves, making up silly British identities for themselves. For example, one woman might decide she's Bromilda Huntington the III, the famous polo player and heir to the immense Huntington fortune. Another woman might be Twila Dolittle Arbuthnot, the beautiful upstart who, despite her questionable past, married into the noble Arbuthnot line.

After everyone is introduced, ask each person to close her eyes and bow her head. Ask the Doctor to open her eyes and point to the one person she would like to save. Tell her to close her eyes again. Then ask the murderers to open their eyes and look around to see who the other murderers are. Tell them to point to the person they are going to murder. Have them close their eyes. Ask the Investigator to open her eyes and point to one person she would like to "investigate." You will then either shake your head "yes," that the person is one of the murderers or "no," that the person is not.

Then ask guests to open their eyes. Announce who has been murdered. (If the Doctor chose to save the same person the murderers tried to kill, announce that someone *tried* to murder that person unsuccessfully.) If someone *is* murdered, that person murdered is now "out" and cannot give any input for the rest of the game. Now ask women to accuse who they think the murderers are. For example, one might say, "I think it's that Twila Arbuthnot; she's been eyeing my jewels all night!" The Investigator can choose to say whom she investigated and whether or not this person was the murderer if it will help save or condemn someone.

Once guests have had time to discuss, take a vote for who among the accused should pay for this crime. Whoever gets the most votes will be "hung" for the murder and will then be out. Have guests close their eyes again and go through the same process as before: Have the Doctor save someone, the murderers kill someone, the Investigator investigate someone; then announce the murder or attempted murder, accuse one another, and vote whom to hang. Play until all of the murderers have been hung or until all guests have been murdered. If all the murderers are accused and hung, the guests win. If all the guests are murdered, the Jenkings Jewelry Ring has triumphed.

Sometimes one side will quickly defeat the other, in which case you can redraw cards. If the murderers win too quickly, have one less murderer. If you want to host more murder mysteries in the future, all you have to do is use the same basic game but create a new story for the case.

Party Tip

Anyone can *say* she's the Investigator, even the murderers. And the murderers might choose to kill the Investigator next if they know who she is so reveal your identity with care!

Party Tip

Don't tell guests whether or not the person hung was the real murderer.

The Mysterious Lover

If you'd like to add a spiritual element to your mystery party, give women clues to unravel about their mysterious lover who is always reaching out to them, Jesus.

1. Type out and tie this verse to their mugs of apple cider: *"[God] determined the times set for [men] and the exact places where they should live. God did this so that men would seek him and perhaps reach out for him and find him, though he is not far from each one of us"* (Acts 17:26-27).

2. Then have this verse sitting at their places as they sit down to eat: *"For since the creation of the world God's invisible qualities—his eternal power and divine nature—have been clearly seen, being understood from what has been made"* (Romans 1:20).

3. Then have this verse tied to the sticks of the caramel apples they create: *"So I say to you: Ask and it will be given to you; seek and you will find; knock and the door will be opened to you. For everyone who asks receives; he who seeks finds; and to him who knocks, the door will be opened"* (Luke 11:9-10).

These verses all point to one truth: God loves us and is seeking us out, trying to draw us to him. He is dropping clues all around us, so we'll catch his scent and chase after him. After women have read the verses, talk with one another about how God drops clues in your lives to draw you close to him. Discuss these questions together:

- God placed you exactly where you are so that you would notice him and reach for him. What in your surroundings draws you to God?

- Is there something God has placed in your midst to draw you to him that you ought to start taking notice of?

- Romans 1:20 says we can see God's qualities by what he has made. What clues does the creation around you give you about what God is like?

- God has left us clues about himself, and he wants us to seek him. In what way could you make an active effort to seek God and knock at his door?

Book Club ·····················

Murder Must Advertise by Dorothy L. Sayers. A classic murder mystery by a great female Christian author (and one of the first female graduates of Oxford!).

Ten Little Indians by Agatha Christie. Another great British murder mystery—a bunch of British folks getting murdered one by one at an English manor. Sound familiar?

In Grandma's Kitchen

It's *almost* the most wonderful time of the year! Get ready by polishing up those homey skills you learned (or never learned) from your grandmother. You and your friends will create show-stopping pie crusts together that they can take home and freeze, then learn to knit fun Christmas gifts, too. And if domestic skill-honing won't draw in your friends by the droves, just lure them with the tasty homecookin'!

- Great party to invite new friends to
- Can work for any size group

Menu ::::::::::::::::::

Pour on the comfort with some of Grandma's holiday favorites. These warm and cozy dishes are so tasty and will remind you of fall days with family—they are some of my family's tried-and-true holiday recipes.

Ginger Snap's Hot Cocoa

My mom (aka Ginger Snap) loved to make this cocoa on the stove to warm us after playing in the snow. If you have this after your meal, serve it with a ginger snap on the side.

- ○ ½ cup Hershey's dark chocolate cocoa
- ○ 1 cup sugar
- ○ ⅔ cup hot water
- ○ 8 cups whole milk
- ○ 1½ teaspoons vanilla extract
- ○ whipped cream

In a saucepan, mix sugar and cocoa; stir in hot water. Cook over medium heat, stirring, until it boils. Boil while stirring for 2 minutes; then pour in milk. Don't boil, but heat until warmed through. Remove from heat and add vanilla. Top each mug with whipped cream. Makes 8 servings.

Dottie Mae's Artichoke Dip

My grandmother always started a party with her famous cheesy artichoke dip.

- ○ 1 cup parmesan cheese
- ○ ½ cup mayonnaise
- ○ 4½-ounce can chopped green chilies
- ○ 15-ounce can artichoke hearts
- ○ bread for dipping

Drain green chilies and artichokes. Tear artichokes into small pieces. Mix all ingredients together. Spread in an 8x8-inch pan and bake at 325 degrees for 30 minutes. Serve with bread chunks.

Party Tip

If you have this party in early November, your friends can be ready for those pies come Turkey Day.

Party Tip

To save time, use the meat from a rotisserie chicken to make this soup (though using all thigh meat makes it much richer!).

Jan's Creamy Chicken Noodle Soup

This is based on a recipe from my sweet editor, Jan Kershner, for one of the tastiest chicken noodle soups I've had.

- ○ 1 pound cooked chicken thighs, skinless and boneless
- ○ 16 cups chicken stock
- ○ 1 large onion, chopped
- ○ 2 medium carrots, chopped
- ○ 2 celery stalks, chopped
- ○ ½ teaspoon pepper
- ○ ½ teaspoon sage
- ○ ½ teaspoon garlic powder
- ○ 1 teaspoon lemon pepper
- ○ 4 tablespoons butter
- ○ ¼ cup flour
- ○ 1½ cups half and half
- ○ 12-ounce package egg noodles (use thick ones, such as kluski noodles)

Combine first nine ingredients in a large pot, and simmer for 45 minutes. In the meantime, prepare noodles according to package directions and set aside. In a saucepan, melt the butter, and whisk in flour. When combined, add half and half and stir until thick. Add to soup with noodles and heat through. (Add more chicken stock at this time if there's not enough liquid.) Serves 10.

Thelma Mae's Angel Biscuits

This specialty of my grandmother's is a nice side to the soup. My husband says he hates biscuits, but even he can't resist these yummy bites.

- ○ 1 package dry yeast
- ○ 2 tablespoons warm water
- ○ 5 cups flour
- ○ ½ cup sugar
- ○ 1 teaspoon baking soda
- ○ 3 teaspoons baking powder
- ○ 1 teaspoon salt
- ○ 1 cup butter
- ○ 2 cups buttermilk

Add yeast to warm water to soften. Sift together next 5 ingredients. Cut butter into ingredients until as coarse as cornmeal. Add 2 cups buttermilk and yeast mixture, and mix. Drop by the spoonful on a baking sheet. Bake 15 to 25 minutes at 350 degrees. Makes about 24 biscuits.

Delma's Herbed Green Bean Casserole

This dish, from my sister-in-law's mother, is a pleasant variation from the traditional green bean casserole you see around this time of year.

- ○ ½ cup dried bread crumbs
- ○ 2 teaspoons basil
- ○ 1 teaspoon oregano
- ○ 1 teaspoon garlic powder
- ○ ½ teaspoon salt
- ○ ½ teaspoon pepper

- ¼ teaspoon thyme
- 1 cup Parmesan cheese, freshly grated
- ⅓ cup vegetable oil
- 16-ounce package frozen cut green beans, cooked to crisp tender

Combine first 8 ingredients in a large bowl. Reserve 3 tablespoons. Add oil and beans and toss to coat. Place in a 1½ quart baking dish. Sprinkle remaining crumbs on top. Bake at 350 degrees for 30 minutes. Serves 8.

Aunt Cin's Apple Pie

My lovely Aunt Cin is always in charge of the pies at our holiday gatherings.

Pie crust
- 2 cups flour, sifted
- 1 teaspoon salt
- ½ cup butter-flavored shortening
- ⅓ cup butter
- ¼ cup ice-cold water

Filling
- 6 cups Granny Smith apples, peeled and sliced
- ¾ cup water
- 1 tablespoon lemon juice
- 2 tablespoons butter
- ¼ teaspoon nutmeg
- ¾ teaspoon cinnamon
- 1 cup sugar
- 2 tablespoons cornstarch

To make crust: Sift the flour and salt together. Add the butter and shortening and cut it together with a fork or pastry blender until in pea-sized pieces. Add water a few drops at a time and toss with a fork. Moisten dough just enough to hold together in a ball. Divide into two balls (one slightly larger than the other) and refrigerate for 30 minutes.

To make filling: In heavy saucepan combine apples, water, lemon juice, butter, and spices. Bring to a boil, and cook until apples are tender. Mix sugar and cornstarch together and add to apples.

Roll out the larger dough on a floured surface until large enough to fit in pan. Trim the edges. Roll out the upper crust. Pour apple mixture into pie crust. Moisten edge of crust with water, and top with second pie crust, cutting slits in the top for steam to escape. Trim the edges and crimp. Bake at 425 degrees for 15 minutes. Reduce heat to 375 degrees and continue baking for another 25 to 30 minutes.

Party Tip

See the perfect pie crust section (page 79) for lots of pie-crust making tips.

Adding Pizzazz

You'll want to provide your guests with a cozy atmosphere that will help them relax and enjoy one another's friendship. (Remember, they may be coming from one of those holiday mall trips!) Re-create the comfort of your grandmother's kitchen with a few easy touches.

- **Light pumpkin-pie or apple-cider scented candles.**

- **Pull out the old pictures** you have of grandparents, great-grandparents, and great-great-grandparents. Set picture frames all around your dining room or meeting area.

- **Use the comfiest seating possible.** Pull any rocking chairs or easy chairs you have into your meeting area.

- **Have an abundance of quilts and blankets** around to make your guests cozy.

- **Tell your guests to bring their slippers** to wear at your party.

- **If you have a fireplace, get it crackling!**

- **Think of your grandmother** (or another person who always created a warm haven for you), and think of what she always did to make her home welcoming, such as having fresh flowers, setting out fresh chocolate chip cookies, wearing a frilly apron, or always having a big hug for her guests. Then do it for your friends!

- **If you'd like to give your friends each a party gift,** give them jars filled with homemade biscotti to dip in their coffee on a cold day. Perfect for comfort! You could also attach a bag of coffee to the jar. This biscotti recipe is my fave.

Cozy Chocolate Cherry Biscotti

- ⅓ cup butter
- ⅔ cup sugar
- ¼ cup dark cocoa powder
- 2 teaspoons baking powder
- 2 eggs
- 1¾ cups flour
- 6 ounces semisweet chocolate chips
- ¼ cup dried cherries, chopped
- chocolate for dipping

Beat butter with an electric mixer for 30 seconds. Add sugar, cocoa, and baking powder, and combine. Beat in eggs; then as much flour as you can. You may need to stir by hand to add all the flour. Stir in chocolate and cherries.

Shape dough into two 10-inch rolls. Place on greased cookie sheet and flatten slightly. Bake for 25 minutes at 375 degrees, until a toothpick comes out clean. Cool for 1 hour.

Cut each roll into ½-inch thick slices. Place, cut side down, on an ungreased cookie sheet. Bake for 8 minutes at 325 degrees. Then turn over and bake 8 more minutes. Once the cookies have cooled, melt chocolate in the microwave and dip one tip of each cookie in the chocolate. Let cool. Makes about 30 cookies.

Bring in the Entertainment!

The Perfect Pie Crust

If you talk to some bakers, making the perfect pie crust seems an art and science as precise and secret as creating a rocket at home. Clear away these secretive mists and help your friends get ready for the holiday season by making pie crusts together. The secrets to a good crust are listed below. Have on hand enough ingredients (or ask your friends to bring ingredients) so that each woman can make one or two pie crusts to take home. Use the pie crust recipe (page 77) listed in the recipe section (which will make two crusts) or use your own secret recipe and integrate the tips listed below for the perfect pie crust.

If you want to feel like you have your own cooking show, demonstrate first how to make the perfect crust. (Or invite your grandmother or another expert you know and have *her* demonstrate!) Then have enough work stations set up for guests to make their own crusts. Your guests can wrap the prepared crusts in wax paper and refrigerate them until they leave. When they get home, they can freeze the crusts to have ready at hand for the holiday pie season. Now, wasn't that more fun than hurriedly making crusts on your own the day of the big event?

Crust Tips

It was uncommon to find recipes for pie crusts in early American cookbooks because pies were so popular, it was just assumed cooks already had their own secret recipe in their arsenal. Well, some of us have forgotten and could use a little help. Here are a few secrets to creating the perfect crust:

- Bake in a glass plate or dull metal plate rather than a shiny metal pie plate, which doesn't allow proper browning.

- Keep your liquids ice cold.

- Keep your fats (shortening, margarine, or butter) chilled. If it's warm, the flour will absorb it, making your crust tough.

- For an extra-buttery crust, use butter-flavored shortening. Cut your fat (butter or shortening) into smaller pieces before adding flour so less blending is needed and fat will melt less.

- Always measure your ingredients carefully—you need just the right balance of flour, fat, and liquid. Too much flour and your crust will be tough. Too much fat and it will be crumbly. Too much liquid and you'll need more flour (making the crust tougher).

- Add your cold water gradually, not all at once, and use the minimum amount necessary.

- Handle the dough as little as possible. The more you work with it, the tougher it will get.

Party Tip

You might want to ask guests to bring rolling pins, pastry blenders, and boards if you don't have enough.

- To keep the bottom of the pie from getting mushy while baking, brush it with beaten egg white before adding filling.

- If topping a pie with a crust, always cut slits for steam to escape from.

Memory Lane

Ask your guests to bring photos of their grandmothers or an older woman who was an important part of their lives. Take turns telling your favorite stories about your grandmothers, what you admired in them, and one thing you learned from them. If you want, you could also use this as a discussion time, using the following questions:

- Tell about an older woman who has been a mentor to you. What did you learn from her?

- Read Titus 2:3-5. Do you have any relationships with women that follow this model? If not, do you wish you did? Why?

- Tell about a time you were able to help mentor another woman.

- Are you in a place where you could be the kind of role model described in Titus 2:3-5 to someone else? If not, how could you get there?

Knitting Pretty

The art of knitting is regaining much of its well-deserved popularity. Revive the social tradition of knitting and chatting while you create Christmas gifts together. A great idea for beginners is a simple scarf. The materials needed are minimal, and a new knitter can make good headway into a project in one night. If you are a veteran knitter or crocheter, you can teach the others the simple steps to create a scarf. If you don't know how, find a friend who does, and recruit her to teach the others. Usually those knitters out there are pretty proud of their craft and eager to pass it on, and it's always easier to learn from a person rather than a book.

If you have skilled friends, they can bring along other projects to work on, too. And it doesn't have to stop there. If you or a friend is a great quilter or sewer or knows any other skill that's now becoming a lost art, pass it on to your friends!

Book Club

Little Women by Louisa May Alcott. A woman could learn a lot about life from these four sisters.

In Grandma's Attic by Arleta Richardson. There's a whole series of "grandma" books by this author, and they're fun to read with daughters and granddaughters, too!

Candy Cane Brunch

Instead of the traditional Christmas tea, this year treat your friends to a candy cane brunch. In December, it's easier to find Saturday mornings your friends are available rather than free Saturday nights. Finding classy decorations to transform your area in a candy-cane land is easy at this time of year, and a brunch will simplify your holiday planning.

- Good for a small or large group of friends
- Easy to prepare before the holidays

Menu ::::::::::::::::::

These dishes are all exceedingly easy, with a touch of holiday flair.

Eggnog Pancakes

Transform simple pancakes with just a little eggnog.

- 2 cups flour
- 3 tablespoons sugar
- 4 teaspoons baking powder
- ¼ teaspoon salt
- ⅛ teaspoon cinnamon
- 2 beaten eggs
- ¾ cup milk
- 1¼ cups eggnog
- ¼ cup cooking oil
- maple syrup

Stir together flour, sugar, baking powder, salt, and cinnamon in a bowl. Make a well in the center and set aside. In another bowl, combine eggs, milk, eggnog, and oil. Add to dry mixture and stir just until moistened (batter will be lumpy).

Cook on a buttered griddle or skillet on medium high. Cook about 2 minutes on each side, until pancakes are golden. (The pancakes will be ready to flip when the tops are covered in bubbles.) Serve with real maple syrup. Serves 8.

Party Tip

This delish dish is a variation of a Christmas-morning tradition of my diva friend Candace McMahan.

Christmas Morning Casserole

This egg casserole just may become your new holiday tradition it's so good.

- 12 ounces breakfast sausage
- ½ yellow onion, chopped
- one 4-ounce can mild green chilies
- ½ cup butter
- ½ cup flour
- 6 eggs
- 1 cup milk
- 1 pound cheddar cheese, cubed
- 2 cups cottage cheese
- 1 teaspoon baking powder
- 1 teaspoon salt
- ¼ teaspoon black pepper
- dash or two of cayenne

Party Tip

If you want, serve the casserole with some buttery sourdough toast.

Brown sausage according to package directions and add onions during last 5 minutes. Add green chilies and set aside. In a small saucepan, melt butter. When melted, add flour and whisk until smooth. In another bowl, beat eggs, and add flour mixture and remaining ingredients. Layer sausage onion mixture on the bottom of a 9x13-inch pan. Pour egg mixture on top. Bake for 45-50 minutes at 350 degrees. Serves 8.

Baked Apples With Cinnamon Stems

Fruit follows a rich brunch well. The cinnamon "stems" in these apples add charm to a simple dessert. Use any firm, tart baking apple.

- 8 medium-sized baking apples, such as Gala, cored
- 24 whole cloves
- 12 dates, coarsely chopped
- ¼ cup dried cherries
- ½ teaspoon cinnamon
- ⅓ cup brown sugar
- 2½ tablespoons butter, cut into small pieces
- eight 2-inch-long cinnamon sticks
- ⅔ cup water or apple cider
- heavy cream

Preheat the oven to 350 degrees. Press 3 whole cloves into the sides of each apple, and place in a shallow baking dish, just large enough to hold apples without touching. Combine the dates, cherries, cinnamon, brown sugar, and butter. Spoon mixture into the center of each apple. Press a cinnamon stick into the center, leaving ½ inch exposed.

Pour the water or cider into the pan. Cover tightly with aluminum foil, and bake for 30 minutes. Remove the aluminum, and baste the apples with the juices. Bake for 10 minutes more, until apples are tender but not mushy. Serve warm or at room temperature. Drizzle heavy cream over the apples before serving. Serves 8.

Party Tip

These snowballs have a shortbread-like consistency. If you like your snowballs nuttier, you can double or even quadruple the amount of pecans. (My husband likes four times the nuts.)

Candy Cane Snowballs

These are my all-time favorite Christmas cookies.

- 1 cup butter
- ½ cup powdered sugar
- 1 teaspoon vanilla
- 2¼ cups flour
- ¼ teaspoon salt
- ¼ cup pecans, ground
- 1 cup powdered sugar
- 5 mini candy canes, ground in a food processor

Mix the ½ cup sugar, vanilla, and butter together. Work in flour, salt, and nuts until dough holds together. (You may not need all the flour.) Shape dough into 1-inch balls. Place on an ungreased baking sheet and bake 10-12 minutes at 400 degrees.

Mix 1 cup powdered sugar with the ground candy canes. While the cookies are still warm, roll in candy cane mixture. Let cool slightly and roll once more.

Chai Nog/Chocolate Nog

The spices of chai tea (cinnamon, nutmeg, ginger) mix well with eggnog and make a fabulous holiday treat. If your guests aren't chai fans, they probably are chocolate fans! Switch out the chai mix for hot cocoa mix.

- ○ 4 cups light eggnog
- ○ 4 cups milk
- ○ ¾ cup chai mix (the concentrate in grocery stores next to the bagged tea)
- ○ peppermint candy stick stirrers

Heat eggnog, milk, and chai tea mix on medium heat until hot. Pour into mugs and serve with peppermint stick stirrers. (If using hot cocoa, put a little bit less than the amount of mix recommended for one cup into the bottom of each cup. Top with the eggnog mixture and stir.) Serves 8.

Adding Pizzazz

- **For simple candy cane elegance, decorate in all reds and whites.**

- **If you have white dishware,** use it complemented by red napkins. You can create easy napkin rings by tying napkins with red or white satin ribbon. Secure one mini candy cane (or two candy canes crossing each other) onto the ribbon by tying them on with a bow.

- **To label each place, buy one round, red ornament per guest.** Write each guest's name on the ornament using a gold or silver paint pen. Set an ornament on the center of each plate.

- **Red roses and peppermint sticks make a striking yet whimsical centerpiece.** Buy a large round piece of floral foam and soak it with water. Place this on a large round dish. Hot glue peppermint sticks vertically all the way around the edge of the foam. Arrange the roses by sticking them into the craft foam. You can use berries and pine sprigs on wire picks as accents to your arrangement or go with just roses.

- **For an easy seasonal centerpiece,** place pomegranates and chestnuts or whole walnuts in a tall cylindrical bowl or large glass bowl.

- **For a simple decoration for a buffet,** place shiny red or white ornaments atop clear, white, or silver candlesticks of varying heights. You can also put red, white, or clear ornaments in a large clear bowl.

- **Scatter unwrapped peppermint candies around your table for a bit of color.** To add a warm glow, place lit votive candles or short white candles on the table.
- **Decorate a mini tree** for your area using all white and red globe ornaments.
- **Use a tiered cookie plate to display lit votive candles,** red and white ornaments, and peppermint candies.
- **Wrap small boxes** in white wrapping paper and red ribbons or vice versa, and place around your party area.
- **If you serve coffee or hot chocolate, use peppermint sticks as stir sticks.**
- **For gifts for your guests,** you could give candy cane cookies, peppermint bark, peppermint-flavored hot chocolate mix, or big candy canes, of course!
- **For fun candy treats for your guests,** visit www.hammondscandies.com. Hammond's has been making traditional candy in Denver since 1920, including filled candy canes, ribbon candy, Christmas lollipops, and peppermint cocoa stirrers.
- **For that last over-the-top touch, burn peppermint-scented candles.**

Bring in the Entertainment!

- **If you're in a smaller group, consider having a small gift exchange.** Each person can bring a gift of about a $5 value, and guests can draw numbers to choose gifts.
- **You can use the candy cane as a vehicle for telling Jesus' story.** Although it's unclear (and much disputed) what the origin of the candy cane was, it has come to symbolize several things at this time of year. Give guests each a candy cane, and tell them of several truths it can remind us of.

  First, the candy cane is formed in the shape of a shepherd's crook. Jesus is our shepherd, watching over us and caring for us. (It's also in the shape of a J when turned over.) Second, the white of the candy cane symbolizes Jesus' purity. He came to this Earth as an innocent child, and remained pure until his death. Last, the red stripes are said to symbolize God's love and Jesus' blood shed for us. Because of God's love for us, he chose to make a pure sacrifice for us in the form of his Son. Through God's incredible gift of his pure Son born into the world, we can be saved from our sins through Jesus' sacrifice.

  You can write out this story of the symbolism of the candy cane on a card to give to each guest, or tell this story during your brunch as a way of sharing the good news with your guests.

- **Read the Christmas story together: Matthew 1:18–2:12; Luke 1:26-56; 2:1-20.** You can have several women do a dramatic reading, have women take turns reading the story, read it yourself, or have verses written out on place cards at each place for women to read in turn. You could also read The Magnificat together, Luke 1:46-55. This song is Mary's response to God for choosing her to be the mother of the Messiah.

This passage can lead to a great discussion of how we choose to respond to difficult situations in our own lives.

- **If you'd like to have a short teaching at your brunch,** base your teaching on a popular Christmas song. We get used to singing certain songs without even noticing the depth of the lyrics. Here are great songs to base a teaching on: "Breath of Heaven" by Amy Grant, "It Came Upon a Midnight Clear," "O Come, O Come, Emmanuel," and "O Holy Night." Before your teaching have a soloist sing the song, and after your teaching, sing the song all together. (If you choose to discuss the song "Breath of Heaven," read The Magnificat together, Mary's response to her situation, Luke 1:46-55.)

- **If you'd like to have a discussion time at your brunch,** write out Christmas verses and questions and attach them to candy canes set at each place. Have each woman read the question and verse attached to her candy cane, and then have women discuss the questions together at their tables. Here are some examples:

  - *"The Word gave life to everything that was created, and his life brought light to everyone. The light shines in the darkness, and the darkness can never extinguish it" (John 1:4-5).*
    How has Jesus brought light into your life?

  - *"Because of God's tender mercy, the morning light from heaven is about to break upon us, to give light to those who sit in darkness and in the shadow of death, and to guide us to the path of peace" (Luke 1:78-79).*
    What is the path of peace referred to in this verse? How has Jesus brought you peace?

  - *"Look! The virgin will conceive a child! She will give birth to a son, and they will call him Immanuel, which means 'God is with us'" (Matthew 1:23).*
    What comfort do you find in Jesus' name, Immanuel?

  - *"Mary responded, 'Oh, how my soul praises the Lord. How my spirit rejoices in God my Savior! For he took notice of his lowly servant girl, and from now on all generations will call me blessed' " (Luke 1:46-48).*
    What can we infer about God, knowing that he chose a humble servant girl to be the mother of his Son?

Book Club

The Best Christmas Pageant Ever by Barbara Robinson. A humorous short Christmas read for the holiday season.

Christ the Lord: Out of Egypt by Anne Rice. A first-person narrative of Jesus' life as a 7-year-old (as his family leaves Egypt and moves to Nazareth), based on the author's historical research.

The Man Born to Be King by Dorothy L. Sayers. A dramatization of Jesus' life, starting with the Christmas story.

"Girls Just Wanna Have Fun" Pajama Party!

• Good anytime, with anyone, at any place!

The holidays are over, and the long cold months and cabin fever are setting in. The best remedy? A pajama party! It's time to get a little silly. Whether your friends stay the night or just stay 'til midnight, get ready to let your hair down and giggle. You can have this party with just a few friends or with a gaggle of women.

Menu

It's time for slumber party food—fun, easy treats you can throw together beforehand in no time or make together at your party.

Party Tip

Carrots and celery taste *way* better when they're crisp and crunchy. Cut your veggies ahead of time, and store them in the fridge immersed in water. Take them out just before your guests arrive.

Veggies and Cheese Dip

Here's a party favorite of my husband's grandmother, perfect for graduation parties, Christmas parties, or pajama parties! Your guests can munch on this when they arrive.

- ○ carrots, sliced
- ○ celery, sliced
- ○ 8-ounce jar Cheez Whiz
- ○ 8-ounce package cream cheese, softened
- ○ 1 teaspoon Worcestershire sauce
- ○ ½ teaspoon celery salt
- ○ ½ teaspoon garlic salt

Mix last 5 ingredients with electric mixer until well blended. Serve with carrots and celery.

California Pizza

If you don't want to make your own crust, buy a premade crust from the store. Make the pizza together so you can all customize.

Crust
- ○ 1¼ cups flour
- ✳ ○ ½ cup whole wheat flour
- ○ 2 tablespoons vegetable oil
- ○ ½ teaspoon salt
- ○ 1 package active dry yeast
- ○ ½ cup warm water
- ○ 1 teaspoon honey
- ○ red pepper flakes

Toppings
- ○ 1 jar prepared pesto
- ○ mozzarella cheese
- ○ feta cheese
- ○ Parmesan cheese
- ○ 1 cup cubed chicken, cooked
- ○ 1 jar artichoke hearts, drained
- ○ 1 jar sun-dried tomatoes, drained
- ○ ½ cup thinly sliced red onions

Party Tip

If you don't have whole wheat flour on hand, you can use all white.

In a large bowl, combine oil, salt, and flours. In a small cup, dissolve yeast in water, and add honey. Add yeast to flour mixture and stir. Knead until smooth. Place in a greased bowl, cover with a damp towel, and let rise until doubled. Knead again lightly, and mix in red pepper flakes, as desired. Roll out on a floured surface to 14 inches.

Spread evenly with pesto. Top with cheeses, chicken, artichokes, sun-dried tomatoes, and red onions as desired. Bake at 475 degrees for 12 to 15 minutes. Makes one 14-inch pizza.

Party Tip

Try rolling your pizza dough into a rectangular shape— it looks nice and rustic that way.

Tara's Strawberry Salad

My sister brings this bright salad to our family parties.

- 2 bags romaine lettuce
- 2 cups strawberries, sliced
- 1 cup mozzarella cubes
- 3 ounces sunflower seeds
- 3 ounces pecans, chopped
- 1 white onion, chopped

Dressing
- 2 teaspoons mustard powder
- 3 tablespoons poppy seeds
- 1½ cups sugar
- ⅔ cup red wine vinegar
- 1½ teaspoons salt
- 1 cup vegetable oil

Mix dressing ingredients in a sealable cup and shake hard until sugar is dissolved. Combine salad ingredients in a large bowl and toss with dressing. Serves 8.

✳ Party Tip

If you can't find good strawberries, substitute chopped apples and dried cranberries or cherries.

Apple Pie Shake

I had my first apple pie shake at The Malt Shop in Estes Park, Colorado. I couldn't believe it when they flat out stuck a piece of apple pie in a blender with some ice cream. But then I tasted it, and they made a believer out of me.

- one frozen apple pie, baked according to package directions and cooled
- vanilla ice cream
- milk
- cinnamon
- nutmeg

For each shake, place one piece of pie in a blender with three scoops of ice cream, ¼ cup milk, 2 dashes cinnamon, and 1 dash nutmeg. Blend. Add more ice cream if too thin and more milk if too thick. Serve in a tall frosty glass (dip glasses in water and store in the freezer).

Winter

Chrissy's Morning After Frappe

If your guests do stay overnight, here's a tasty smoothie to wake you up the morning after, courtesy of my sis.

- ○ one 12-ounce can frozen grape juice concentrate
- ○ 2 large bananas
- ○ ½ cup frozen blueberries
- ○ 2 cans cold water
- ○ 4 cups crushed ice
- ○ lime slices for garnish

Blend first 4 ingredients in a blender until smooth. Add ice and blend just until snowy. Serves 8.

Adding Pizzazz

- **Get your little hands on a Cyndi Lauper CD,** preferably *She's So Unusual,* which has "Girls Just Want to Have Fun" on it (the first tape I ever owned, incidentally; I must have been born to have fun). It will get your party started. Or pick the best party music from your generation (or the majority of your guests' generation). Hearing their old high school faves will get your friends in the party mood.

- **Another great way to have great tunes at your party and for a party favor:** Ask each of your friends what her all-time favorite song is (party song, dance song, whatever). Then create a mix CD to play during the night, and give the CD as a party favor to each guest. (Buy the MP3s online on a site such as iTunes.) Each time they listen to it, they'll remember the fun time you had.

- **By all means, have your friends come in their pj's and slippers** (or have them change when they get there). Make sure your heat is turned up so your friends' tootsies don't freeze.

- **Greet your guests at the door with candy necklaces;** if they're not ready to have fun yet, it's only a matter of time before the sugar high kicks in.

- **Light sugar cookie–scented candles** for a warm and yummy welcome for your friends.

- **If you want to go with a girlie theme,** use all pink and purple decorations. Use balloons, streamers, paper plates, and napkins.

- **Have lots of pillows and blankets** around so everyone can wrap up. (And get into pillow fights, of course.)

Bring in the Entertainment!

There are oodles of fun party activities that need no explanation from me. Here's a list of ideas to get your creative juices flowing:

- pillow fight
- Twister
- spa night (with face masks and pedicures)
- karaoke
- scrapbooking night
- trampoline competition
- play favorite childhood games, such as Monopoly and Life
- freeze one another's bras (just kidding)

Sometimes the most simple and silly entertainment is the most fun. Think scooter races down the halls of your church…the game of Sardines (where one person hides, and when you find the person, you hide there, too, until your whole party is stuffed in a closet)…kidnapping your pastor's lawn flamingo and taking pictures of your fun adventures with it (slide show the following Sunday optional).

Movie Night

You can't have a pajama party without a movie, right? Here are some of my favorite slumber party movies to turn on when you're all getting droopy eyed:

Pride and Prejudice (the *fabulous* 2005 movie or the 5-hour miniseries for you die-hard fans)
The Parent Trap (with Hayley Mills or the version with Lindsay Lohan)
Return to Me
Pillow Talk (1959 flick with Doris Day and Rock Hudson)
Ever After
The Princess Bride

Truth or Dare

For as long as I've been going to pajama parties, the idea of playing Truth or Dare always comes up. We start with good intentions, but more often than not, the game's a bust—no one can think of any good truths or dares. So your game doesn't bust, I've done the thinking for you. This game is a great way to learn things you never knew about your friends. Just write out the truths or dares below on slips of paper and put them in a Truth hat and a Dare hat. Have women take turns picking truth or dare. If you'll have a large group, come up with some more truths and dares! Add or omit these suggestions based on the demographics of your group (Don't ask your 82-year-old friend to do a cartwheel.)

Truth

- What do you want to be when you grow up? (Dream big here—if you could be anything you wanted, what would you be?)

- Which would you rather do: swim in a river full of snakes (friendly, nonpoisonous snakes, of course), eat a big juicy cockroach, or cliff dive from a 100-foot cliff?

- If you could be any famous person, who would you be? Why?

Winter

- What's your favorite memory from elementary school? (Can't remember that far back? How about middle or high school?)

- What virtue do you think God blessed you with an extra serving of? What one virtue do you think you could use a whole lot more of?

- Say your favorite thing about one other person in the room. (For example, "I love Jen's laugh," or "My favorite thing about Sarah is her honesty.")

- What's your least favorite thing about church? Why? What could you do to make this thing change?

- What's your favorite characteristic of God? (His sense of humor, his patience, his love.) Why?

Dare

- Sing "Supercalifragilisticexpialidocious" in your manliest voice. (Don't know it? You're not off the hook; have the person on your left pick another song for you to sing bass to.)

- Demonstrate for the group how you danced in high school. Was it the Mashed Potato? the Hand-Jive? the Cabbage Patch? the Snake?

- Do your very best Marilyn Monroe impersonation—and it has to last at least 30 seconds. (Don't know Marilyn's mannerisms? Have the person on your left pick another person for you to impersonate.)

- Eat 10 saltine crackers in one minute. (It's not as easy as it sounds.)

- Put your forehead on a bat touching the ground, spin in a circle 10 times, and then attempt to do three somersaults in a row…followed by your best cartwheel.

- Get out the timer and name as many of the 50 states as you can in one minute.

- It's time for Charades. Get everyone to guess the title of this movie using no words: *Who Framed Roger Rabbit?*

Book Club ::::::::::::::::::

The Sisterhood of the Traveling Pants by Ann Brashares. Four high school friends are bound by a seemingly magical pair of pants. (I know, I know: It's for high schoolers. But I know women well past 18 who eat this stuff up, myself included. And friendship is friendship, whether you're 18 or 80.)

The Princess Bride by William Goldman. Yes, you've probably seen the movie, but the book is even more fun.

Girl-About-Town Cosmopolitan Bash

I've always wanted to be a little bit like Audrey Hepburn—sophisticated at parties in her little black dress, oozing with confidence and wit. OK, so maybe that's my vanity speaking, but at *your* cosmopolitan bash, you can play up all the great parts of a black dress party—getting to meet and make new friends and experiencing and appreciating culture. Take your party whichever direction you prefer: an appetizer party at your pad for your friends to get to know each other before a night out, or a night in where you and your friends explore expressions of faith through art. Your bash can be whatever you want it to be!

- Can be done with any size group
- Great party for an alternative worship night

Menu

Instead of a sit-down dinner, celebrate your bash with fun and easy appetizers. Start with the Cuban Spritzer, and then (to make your guests feel extra pampered), serve the appetizers one at a time in an h'ors d'oeuvres pass. (Recruit some guys or teenagers to serve as waiters—hey, maybe they'll even cook for you!) Having the appetizers brought out one by one will encourage lots of mingling! And I'm guessing none of your guests has ever experienced a honey tasting before. After your night of activities, you can end with the ever-classy poached pear.

Party Tip

This party would be a great way to chase away the cold-weather blues in February, *and* it's a great excuse to dress up around Valentine's Day.

Cuban Spritzer

This drink is a refreshing, chic start to your party. You can set up a drink station with instructions so guests can make their own drink.

- ○ crushed ice
- ○ 2 packages fresh mint sprigs
- ○ 3 cups lime juice
- ○ 1½ cups sugar syrup (recipe follows)
- ○ 2 cups club soda

To make a glass: Place several mint leaves in a glass and bruise with a wooden spoon. To each glass, add 3 ounces lime juice and 1½ ounces sugar syrup, and stir. Fill the glass with ice, and add 1-2 ounces club soda. Serves 8.

Sugar Syrup

- ○ 3 cups water
- ○ 3 cups sugar

In a saucepan, stir together water and sugar over medium heat. Stir until sugar dissolves. Bring to a boil, reduce heat, and simmer 5 minutes, stirring occasionally. Refrigerate syrup until cold. (Will keep in fridge up to a month.) Makes about 4 cups.

Finger Food

For your appetizers, think simple, quality, and store-bought. Here are some ideas.

- olives (try a new kind from the olive bar)
- melon balls wrapped in prosciutto slices
- dried apricots stuffed with Gorgonzola
- baguette slices topped with smoked salmon slices and fresh dill
- pear slices topped with brie
- cucumber rounds topped with hummus
- baguette slices rubbed with garlic cloves, toasted with olive oil, and topped with roasted red peppers
- dates wrapped with bacon and broiled for 10-12 minutes, turning once

Party Tip

Get creative with toppings on these fun bites; stack with pesto, olives, tomato slices, mini-mozzarella balls, and basil leaves; it'll take these tasty snacks to new heights of sophistication.

Toasted Ravioli

- one 9-ounce package refrigerated ravioli
- 2 eggs, beaten
- 1 cup Italian-seasoned dry bread crumbs
- ½ teaspoon salt
- cooking spray
- Parmesan cheese
- marinara sauce, warmed
- various toppings

Prepare ravioli according to package directions. Mix bread crumbs and salt in a small bowl. Dip ravioli into beaten eggs; then coat with bread crumbs. Place on a greased baking sheet. Spray with cooking spray. Broil for 2 minutes; then flip them over. Spray with additional cooking spray and broil for 1 minute, or until lightly browned. Grate Parmesan over ravioli, and serve with heated marinara sauce. Top as desired with pesto, tomatoes, olives, and so on. Makes approximately 45 raviolis.

Crab and Mango Bites

Dressing
- 1 medium Fuji apple, chopped
- 1 small garlic clove, chopped
- 2 tablespoons cider vinegar
- ¾ teaspoon salt
- ½ cup olive oil

Salad
- 1 pound crab meat
- 1 large mango, chopped
- 1 medium Fuji apple, chopped
- 1½ tablespoons fresh cilantro, chopped
- endive leaves

To make dressing: Mix first 4 dressing ingredients in a blender until very smooth. Add oil slowly with motor running, about 30 seconds.

To make salad: Combine crab, apple, mango, cilantro, and 6 tablespoons of dressing. Season with salt. Put a heaping spoonful of salad on each endive leaf. Drizzle the platter with remaining dressing.

Party Tip

If you can't get your hands on good crab meat, substitute chopped or shredded cooked chicken— fake crab just won't do the other tasty ingredients justice.

Onion and Camembert Tarts

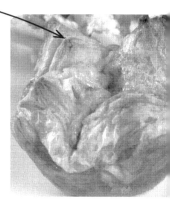

Camembert is a creamy French cheese, similar to Brie.

- one 17.3-ounce package frozen puff pastry (2 sheets), thawed
- 1 tablespoon butter
- 3 cups chopped yellow onions
- salt
- ⅔ cup whipping cream
- 4 ounces Camembert cheese, cut in ½-inch pieces
- 1 large egg
- pinch of cayenne
- pinch of nutmeg
- ¼ cup freshly grated Parmesan cheese

Preheat oven to 400 degrees. Melt butter in a large skillet over medium heat. Add onions, and cook until tender, about 10 minutes. Season with salt, and set aside to cool. In a medium saucepan, bring cream to a simmer over medium heat. Reduce heat to low and add Camembert, stirring until melted. Cool 5 minutes; then whisk in egg, cayenne, and nutmeg. Set aside.

Cut each thawed puff pastry sheet into nine squares. Press squares into muffin tins, forming tarts. Spread the onions over this. Drizzle custard evenly over tarts. Sprinkle Parmesan evenly over tarts. Bake 15 minutes, or until lightly browned. Cool on a wire rack 10 minutes. Serve warm. (These can be made ahead of time and briefly reheated in the oven.) Makes 18 tarts.

Honey Tasting

What hoity-toity appetizer party would be complete without some sort of tasting? Finish your h'ors d'oeuvres course with a honey tasting. There are over 300 varieties of honey available in the U.S., and most of your guests probably never have tasted any side by side. Discover together the delicacies of honey—you can find many excellent local honeys that each have their own personality. For each variety of honey, give women half of a water cracker, a baguette slice, or a mild fruit, such as pear slices, dabbed with the honey. Discuss together what each one tastes like and which is your favorite. (You could even offer the dessert, the poached pears, drizzled with everyone's favorite honey warmed up.) You can also provide honeycomb, cut into bite-size pieces, and have each woman give it a try. Here are some ideas for what you can offer:

- water crackers (broken in half and dabbed with a small amount of honey)
- fruit slices
- alfalfa honey (mild, good table honey)
- avocado honey (rich and buttery)
- buckwheat honey (strong and distinct)
- clover honey (delicate, the most common honey)
- orange blossom honey (light flavor with the aroma of orange blossoms)
- honeycomb (cut into bite-size pieces)

Party Tip

Use any extra Camembert as an appetizer with fruit.

Party Tip

You can also ask your guests to each bring a type of honey to the party.

Party Tip

Discuss the benefits of honey during your tasting: It's a great substitute for sugar. It's almost one and a half times sweeter than sugar, so you can use less. It also adds distinct flair to whatever you add it to. And, in buying honey, you can often support local businesses and environmentally friendly production.

Poached Pears
With Chocolate Sauce

This dessert is so elegant because of its simplicity.

- ○ 8 Bosc pears
- ○ lemon juice
- ○ 1½ cups sugar
- ○ 2½ cups water
- ○ 1½ teaspoons vanilla

Chocolate sauce

- ○ 6 tablespoons sugar
- ○ 1 cup water
- ○ ¼ cup dark cocoa
- ○ 2 teaspoons cornstarch
- ○ 2 teaspoons vanilla

Peel pairs, and brush lightly with lemon juice. Combine water, sugar, and vanilla, and bring to a boil. (If your pears won't fit in your pan, cook in two batches.) Reduce heat to medium and add the whole pears. Simmer until pears are cooked through, pierced easily with a fork (time will vary). Cool in the liquid, and serve warm or at room temperature, standing on individual plates. Drizzle with chocolate sauce. (Pears can be made ahead of time.) Serves 8.

For chocolate sauce: Combine ingredients in a medium saucepan and mix well. Cook over medium heat, stirring constantly until thickened. Pour over pears.

Adding Pizzazz

With just a few touches, you can transform your party area into a modern, cosmo space perfect for your appetizer party.

- **Clear all clutter from your party area.** Minimal furniture and décor is best.

- **Hang white twinkle lights from the ceiling to create great mood lighting.** If you're having your party at your home, have several rooms open for your friends to mingle in. Use candles or twinkle lights to guide guests to different areas of your place. Place votive candles in the bottom of tall clear plastic glasses to serve as safe guides.

- **For simple and elegant decorations,** place several white calla lilies in tall, slender vases on coffee tables. Silk calla lilies also look very realistic; surround them with river stones in a cylindrical vase.

- **Have you ever looked at modern art and said, "I could have painted *that*"?** Well, here's your big chance. Create abstracts to hang on your walls (enlist the help of a 2-year-old!). Get large white, black, orange, or red pieces of poster board and paints. On one you might paint a big black circle. On another, go for the splatter look. Have your dog step in paint and walk on another. Unleash your inner modern artist. Who knows—maybe you'll discover that your cocker spaniel is the next Picasso.

- **Go for straight lines in the furniture** you scatter around your party area. Instead of that old sagging couch, replace it with four straight chairs.

- **Serve on mismatched dishes of different shapes and sizes.** A red square plate. A polka-dot bowl. A black oval. Perfect.

- **Serve appetizers,** such as olives or melon balls wrapped in prosciutto, in martini or margarita glasses.

- **Have your friends come dressed in cocktail attire.** If you have men or teenagers to serve as your waiters, have them dress in black-tie attire, too.

- **Some jazz playing in the background** would create the right atmosphere. Or, if you have a piano and a piano-playing teenager, enlist his help to create the right ambience.

- **For an extra-sophisticated touch,** light lemongrass-scented candles or other earthy scents, such as sandalwood.

Bring in the Entertainment!

On the Town

If you want, you can have your party be a launching pad for a night on the town. Set out for the art galleries, museums, concerts, poetry readings, or whatever's kicking in your town. After your night of culture, you can head on back to your place for dessert to finish off the evening. If you want to keep your party simple, stick to this basic format and it would be a great party to invite new people to and get to know them.

Expressions of Faith

If you'd prefer to stay in for the evening, have a time of faith expression at your place. When you invite your guests, ask them to consider how they love to express their faith in and love for God. One woman might love to sing, another dance, another write poetry, another scrapbook, another paint. Ask them if they would consider sharing their faith expressions with others at your party. After appetizers, set up an area for your guests to share their expressions (kinda like an open mic night). Some might want to read journal entries, others may sing, others may display art, others may read poetry.

Leave it totally open—you'll be surprised what your friends come up with. It'll take a lot of trust for some to express themselves in front of others, so start off the night by sharing yourself. Make it a safe atmosphere where any can feel free to share by setting up one vital ground rule: Everyone respects every other person's personal expression to God. After everyone has had a chance, spend some time in prayer. Thank God that he listens and enjoys your worship and created each of you to glorify him in a unique way.

Party Tip

I experienced a worship night like this with a small group of people. It's amazing what new things you'll learn about people (I never knew so-and-so plays the harmonica!), and you'll be inspired by the ways others express worship to God.

Party Tip

⋮ Visit Christians in the
⋮ Visual Arts at
⋮ www.civa.org to
⋮ find out about art
⋮ exhibits in your area,
⋮ contemporary artists,
⋮ and for articles on the
⋮ arts, culture, and
⋮ the church.

Art Experience

So much of the great art out there was created as an expression of worship to God. Take time to experience such art at your party and consider the themes the artists were intending to express. Choose several different works of art and obtain prints or pictures of them (some Internet sites sell images of popular art for a small fee that you can download and print out). Display them in several different locations or in one room of your party. Have your guests take time to really experience them—they can observe in silence or discuss with one another how the works affect them. If there's an exhibit in town that's an expression of faith or worship, visit it together and dialogue with one another about your experience.

Here are some artworks to consider together: Michelangelo's "Pietà," a sculpture of Mary holding Jesus' body after the Crucifixion; Notre Dame de Paris, the gorgeous cathedral constructed from 1163 to about 1300; "The Elevation of the Cross" by Rubens, a painting from the 1600's of the raising of Christ on the cross. Your friends' shared insights will open your eyes to new spiritual perspectives and help you deepen your friendships.

Book Club

Confessions of a Shopaholic by Sophie Kinsella. Because sometimes you just need to read some light, fluffy chick lit.

A New Kind of Christian by Brian D. McLaren. A look at Christianity in postmodern times. This book shook up my world.

The Next Generation: Contemporary Expressions of Faith by Wayne Roosa and Patricia C.